GW01607928

Westcott Price Guide To

Advertising Water Jugs & Associated Collectables

Volume Two

In memory of

Jeffery Reardon

1952 - 1999

Published by Westcott Publications
P.O. Box 245
Deniliquin NSW 2710 Australia
Telephone: (03) 5881 2200 Fax: (03) 5881 4740
International:
Telephone: 0011 613 5881 2200 Fax: 0011 613 5881 4740

Published November 1999

Westcott, David.

Westcott Price Guide to Advertising Water Jugs and Associated Collectables, Volume Two.

Includes index

ISBN 0 9577 654 01

FRONT COVER: Top, left to right: "Gilmour Thomson's Scotch Whiskies" tin serving tray, 40 x 30cm (16 x 12″), AUS $400-500; US $250-300; £160-180. "Johnnie Walker" plaster compound figure, 39cm (15½″) high, AUS $500-600; US $300-360; £200-240. "King George IV" rubber compound figure, 37cm (14½″) high, AUS $350-400; US $225-275; £140-165. "Bonnie Prince Charlie Drambuie" rubber compound figure, 33cm (17″) high, AUS $400-500; US $275-325; £150-200.

Centre, left to right: "Buchanan's Special Red Seal" Frank Beardmore & Co., Fenton, 20cm (8″), AUS $3000-3500; US $2000-2500; £1250-1500. "The McCallum" miniature size character jug, no base mark, 7cm (2¾″), AUS $200-250; US $125-150; £80-100. "Dewar's White Label Whisky" John Maddock, 9cm (3½″), AUS $250-300; US $150-180; £100-120. "Dewar's" lead compound miniature figure with matchbox receptical inside base, 12cm (4¾″), AUS $300-350; US $200-230; £120-140. "King's Liqueur Finest Scotch Whisky" change tray, W.T. Copeland & Sons, 15 x 8cm (6 x 3¼″), AUS $375-425; US $240-270; £150-170. "Bulloch Lade Pedigree Scotch Whisky" ashbowl, Shelley, 12.5cm (5″) dia, AUS $300-350; US $180-210; £120-140.

Front, left to right: "Dawson's Scotch Whisky" ashbowl, Causton, 12cm (4¾″) wide x 4 cm (1½″) high, AUS $225-250; US $145-160; £90-100. "Buchanan's Whisky" matchstriker, R. Hammersley & Son, Burslem, 9cm (3½″) high, AUS $800-1000; US $500-650; £325-400. Buchanan's Black & White" Scotch Whisky ashbowl, Shelley, 5.5cm (2″) high, AUS $400-450; US $250-300; £150-180.

Acknowledgements

I am particularly grateful to the following people whose assistance, information, professionalism and friendship created an ideal environment in which to shape this book.

Sydney: Tony Lalor
Terry Hutchinson

Brisbane: Bruce Slade
Dan Martin

Perth: Les Musgrave

Victoria: Graham Gilbert
Wayne Lock

UK: Gordon Litherland
Jon Gray
Alan Blakeman

USA: Milton Kubat

NZ: Rob Dove
Warren Roberts

Denmark: Voigt Madsen

Belgium: Eric Defruytier

"TEACHER'S The Right Spirit Boys" article was re-printed with permission from: Tucker Seabrook Pty Ltd - Wine Spirit & Liqueur Importers & Merchants.

Research and Editorial: David Westcott

Sub Editor: Natasha Bathgate

Literary Consultant: Ron McLucas

Photography: Christopher Maait, David Westcott

Word Processing: Chris van Zeyl

Correspondence: Marlene Westcott

Design and Graphics: Richard Howell
The Magic Lantern Company

Publication Management: Matthew van Zeyl - Studio Image

Special thanks to Diane and Ian for their confidence in my knowledge and ability.

Published by Westcott Publications.

Printed by PRINTBOUND PTY LTD, Blackburn, Victoria, Australia

ISBN 0 9577 654 01

Table of Contents

Foreword

There is an old but true saying we often hear –"Good things come to those who wait."

It probably applies to all of us with a passion for collecting. We are often "waiting" for that one piece to complete a collection; or waiting for that special piece to take us off on a tangent.

Well, in my opinion, this book was worth the wait – far too long for many, but never soon enough for most. The knowledge, research and effort poured in by our Local "International Expert," David Westcott, can only be described as huge! Under very trying conditions, David's decision to regain full control of this Guide has resulted in a more comprehensive, wider ranging and exceptionally professional publication.

Beautifully bound, in full colour and truly international, the information contained in this Guide, has never been researched or presented better by anyone anywhere else world wide.

I, along with many other collectors and supporters of David, am pleased to see this invaluable reference Guide published and can only hope that volumes three, four and five follow in the same professional and informative way in the near future.

Tony Lalor

Introduction

Nine years have passed since I published my first book on advertising water jugs. The book was a best seller in Australia and is now recognised internationally as the "bible" for all jug collectors.

In 1991 the hobby was in its infancy and prices were fluctuating violently from country to country and in many instances there were big gaps between prices being paid in Australia and the US or UK. Prices recently have stabilised and excitingly the number of collectors saving jugs and associated items has, at the very least, trebled. Demand in all categories is now at an all time high.

The popularity of old jugs has always been strong for very good to mint examples. However, recently it has become evident that condition is no longer as important as it was and as a result, small chips and cracks are becoming more acceptable for jugs produced prior to 1940.

Old jugs are not the only ones to become caught up in the whirlwind. For ages it seemed that modern jugs (ie, those produced during the past twenty years) were ignored by collectors, but as supply of the older types has dried up these jugs have come into their own and I have noticed a recent surge in interest. As a result, during the past twelve months prices have increased by about 25% for these types.

I would like to make it quite clear that the prices indicated in this guide are not a "wish list." The majority are prices which I personally have attained through my various auctions and sales. Other prices have been taken from recently held auctions in New Zealand and the United Kingdom.

As the interest in jugs has increased, so too has the interest in accompanying advertising items. Collectors are now searching for related items such as ashtrays, bar figures, match strikers and decanters to enhance the character of their collections. Because of this I have included a range of these items in this guide.

These additional categories of collectables add a new dimension to the hobby because their inclusion not only adds variety to a collection, but tends to make it more attractive and complete. The incorporation of UK pounds and US dollars as well as Australian dollars will make it easier for collectors internationally to use this guide.

David Westcott

"BLACK & WHITE"
SCOTCH WHISKY
"My Never Failing Friends"
"BLACK & WHITE"
SCOTCH WHISKY
HONEST
FRIENDS
LOGAN
"BLACK & WHITE"
Black & White
'BLACK & WHITE'
SCOTCH WHISKY
SCOTCH
BLACK & WHITE
BUCHANAN'S
'BLACK & WHITE'
BUCHANAN'S
BUCHANAN'S
BUCHANAN'S
1840-1940
BUCHANAN'S
"BLACK & WHITE"
WHISKY
BUCHANAN'S
WHISKY
BLACK & WHITE

"BLACK & WHITE"
BLACK & WHITE SCOTCH
BUCHANAN'S
"BLACK & WHITE"
"BLACK & WHITE"
Johnnie Walker Red

The Best of Black & White

Tony Lalor was again a major contributor of material for the second volume of our Water Jug Book. He is featured here at home with part of his extensive collection.

Previous page: Collection of "Buchanan's Black & White" whisky items beside large Johnnie Walker figure.

Top: Tray "My Never Failing Friends" AUS $500-650; US $300-350; £200-230. Tray "Honest Friends" AUS $500-650; US $300-350; £200-230. Tray Eagle With Prey, AUS $600-700; US $400-500; £250-300.

Cabinet top: Brentleigh Ware figure with bottle, AUS $300-350; US $185-225; £120-140. Giant rubber compound figure, AUS $1700-2000; US $1000-1250; £650-750. Matchbox holder, AUS $600-750; US $400-450; £250-300. Tray "Still Watchers" AUS $500-650; US $300-350; £200-250. Bar Figure with bottle, AUS $500-650; US $300-350; £200-250.

Interior of cabinet, top shelf: Ashbowl, AUS $400-450; US $250-300; £150- 180. Jug AUS $400-450; US $260-290; £160-180. Jug, Setter with Bird, AUS $3500-4000; US $2250-2550; £1400-1600. Jug "Good Spirits" AUS $3500-4000; US $2250-2550; £1400-1600. Jug "Grand Spirits" AUS $4500-5000; US $2900- 3200; £1800-2000. Jug "Still Watchers" AUS $3500-4000; US $2250-2550; £1400-1600. Jug, Eagle with Prey, AUS $3500-4000; US $2250-2550; £1400- 1600. Jug, Dogs Running, AUS $400-450; US $260-290; £160-180. Ashbowl, shield t'mark, AUS $250-300; US $130-160; £80-100.

Interior of cabinet, bottom row: "Buchanan's Black & White" jugs with matching ashtrays: Dogs sitting: jug, AUS $600-700; US $375-450; £240-280. Ashtray, AUS $75-100; US 50-65; £30-40. "N.Z. Centennial Exhibition" jug AUS $1000-1250; US $650-800; £425-475. Ashtray, AUS $400-500; US $250-300; £170-200. Shield: jug, AUS $500-600; US $325-365; £200-240. Ashtray, AUS $140-180; US $90-120; £55-65. Dogs with bottle: jug, AUS $650-750; US $425-485; £250-280. Ashtray, AUS $250-300; US $150-180; £100-120. Oval Chequerboard: jug, AUS $600-700; US $375-450; £240-280. Ashtray, AUS $150- 200; US $100-130; £60-80. Oval portrait: jug, AUS $600-700; US $375-450; £240-280. Ashtray, AUS $175-225; US $110-140; £70-90. Hopscotch: jug, AUS $600-700; US $375-450; £240-280. Ashtray, AUS $200-250; US $130-160; £80- 100. Dogs Begging: jug, AUS $650-750; US $425-485; £250-280. Ashtray, AUS $200-250; US $130-160; £80-100.

Extreme right: Giant fibre compound figure of Johnnie Walker, 173cm (5'8") high, AUS $4500-5500; US $2900-3500; £1800- 2200.

Old Jugs, Old Friends & Stories

For several years now I have owned second hand shops and from time to time have had the odd water jug pass through my hands. They have always caught my eye – as advertising jugs are supposed to. Each time it occurred to me that I should keep them. How I wish I had, especially the large cranberry Robertson's Whisky glass jug that I sold for $30 a few years ago! Some people have all the luck, don't they!

Three years ago I started collecting in earnest, I am amazed at how many items I have accumulated in such a short time and the number of other collectors and their spouses I have met along the way. I'm regularly in touch with the United States and Australia and am having a lot of fun talking and swapping jugs and other items.

At present I collect most things to do with whisky advertising. However, I realise that unless I want to live in a barn I will have to specialise during the future.

I realise the older pieces will accelerate more quickly in value but I still can't decide if I like them or the modern pieces for their colours and shapes. Each piece, old or new , is still a thrill to find if I don't already have it.

Recently I sold thirty of my jugs to buy an expensive one, I was happy to have and appreciate it but felt terrible when I looked at my shelves and saw all the empty spaces. It was as though old friends and their stories were gone for good.

I'm in the Auckland phone book and am always happy to talk about jug hunting and swapping as well as meeting new collectors – so get in touch if you wish.

Rob Dove, Auckland, New Zealand

It's Good Therapy

My collecting days began in much the same way as many others. During a celebration my friend and cousin Ron Shipley presented me with a modern Black and White jug. Nothing exciting, just a Wade PDM but it was enough to spark my enthusiasm for this line of collecting.

About that time the Penny Saver magazine was a great source of information for any serious collector so I became an instant subscriber and managed to find some early contacts. Through these contacts my collection began to take on some dimension.

In early 1973 a few devoted collectors formed the New South Wales Jug Club. Like all new clubs everyone had the interest at heart and was keen to improve their own collection and develop the club's activities to benefit all concerned. During those first 12 months I met a host of other collectors and my jug collection grew.

When the club folded it was not a total loss. The contacts I had gathered provided great support in my early collecting years. Tony Lalor was one such friend.

If there is one piece of advice I would pass on to collectors it would be my firm and absolute belief that whatever you put into this hobby has a definite boomerang effect – it does come back to you.

There have been occasions when I have given jugs to new collectors and years later these same people have called with information regarding jugs for sale in places collectors don't usually investigate. The markets are another source that have proven worthwhile with items often available at meagre prices.

In the last few years my list of contacts has increased to worldwide dimensions. My collection has also expanded to include advertising statues, bar mirrors and match strikers, in fact any unusual piece of brewery paraphernalia.

Today I enjoy looking over a collection which represents tireless effort, constant searching and heart wrenching tales of the one that got away. But the nostalgic effect and timeless therapy make it all worthwhile. Successful hunting to all.

Terry Hutchinson, Sydney, Australia

Label
GOLDEN EAGLE
SCOTCH WHISKY
McNISH
McNISH
RODERICK DHU
USHER'S
WHISKY
HARVEY'S
GOLD LABEL
SCOTCH WHISKY
AINSLIE'S
WHISKY
WHITE HORSE
WHISKY
SCOTLAND
LOWRIE
DAWSON'S
SCOTCH WHISKY
USHER'S
Scotch Whisky
OLD MULL
DAWSON
KILMARNOCK
WHISKY
Scotch Whisky
King George IV

Collecting in the States

When I began collecting whisky water jugs for a friend I never dreamed that sixteen years down the track I would have a collection of jugs numbering well over 1500. I went to flea markets, antique shops and garage sales in search of new and different jugs and by the time I had gathered thirty I realised I had the start of a good collection.

Today I have 1550 jugs and they are all on display in the basement of my East Rockaw home.

Here in America jugs are no longer used by restaurants and bars. I have found quite a few during my overseas travels, especially in Spain where I go from bar to bar trading or swapping but rarely selling. My advice to collectors is to carry a few jugs in the boot of your car at all times. Check out every hotel or bar to see if they have any at home to trade, sell or buy. One good source here in America is the Water Pitcher Collectors Association of America (WPCAA) annual "Jugavention."

Milton Kubat, East Rockaw, NY, USA

Beauty...in the eye of the Beholder!

My introduction to the world of whisky water jug collecting started some years ago when a friend gave me an older Black and White Buchanan for Christmas. In those days jugs were readily available from most antique fairs. It soon became obvious you needed to specialise somewhat in the more famous brands. Today's collecting has changed considerably with the better jugs only becoming available through auction. For the new and young collector this can be a problem.

I do not go along with the theory that latter day jugs are not worth handling. Some of the recent auctions prove this point. Any collector worth his salt collects for the love of the challenge not the future value of his jug, although it is a nice thought. Hence the quote "beauty is in the eyes of the beholder."

It's a great hobby and there is still a lot to be learned out there with plenty of scope for everyone.

Jon Gray, Twickenham, Middlesex, England

A Sobering Experience!

I am one of those lucky guys who has a job which is also my main interest – good food, wine and spirits. After completing an apprenticeship I spent a number of years as a bartender on a cruise line travelling all over the world. Sadly, that was before I started collecting commercial jugs. In the beginning, about twenty five years ago, I collected anything with a message on it related to pubs. Now, due to lack of space, I only collect water jugs and other whisky related items.

Together with my wife, who is a great support in collecting and cleaning the jugs, I live in a small town on the outskirts of Copenhagen – Hillerod, population 48,000.

I have worked all my life in Copenhagen's leading restaurants. Until one year ago I was beverage manager in Copenhagen's biggest hotel where I had worked for seventeen years. I have now started a new job as leader of Hillerod's biggest wine shop and after finding my feet have increased sales and now arrange wine tasting seminars.

Besides my collection of water jugs and other whisky items I also have close to 260 different whisky brands (only a few of them not to be opened) and around forty top labels from French brandy, among every other kind of liqueur used in a professional bar. The art which outlasts a human lifetime gives collectors an insight into the past as well comfort and good spirit for the present and future.

In this, the second volume of "Advertising Water Jugs" David Westcott has made a conscientious effort to tabulate, display and valuate these fascinating and beautiful collectable.

With more that twenty years experience as a collector and dealer David is unequalled in his knowledge of water jugs and their value. The first edition, published in 1991, was a fantastic success and I wish David all the best for this new edition. His exhaustive and comprehensive efforts make this a "must read" for collectors.

Voigt Madsen, Hillerod, Denmark

Always made time!

We were bitten by the collecting bug some twenty years ago.

A friend who was a collector started us off with a "Queen Anne" jug by Wade. It was nothing extra special - just a jug with a Queen on it and we were off!

Peggy started writing to distilleries in the United Kingdom and had a good response – quite a few jugs were sent free of charge. For others we had to send back cheques. This proved a very successful exercise and our collection grew rapidly.

I was travelling around Western Australia with my work and always made time to visit antique shops I found. Often they didn't know what a whisky jug was but I found a lot and soon had to slow down or our collection would have grown too big for our house!

We spent our long service leave touring the United Kingdom and visited many small distilleries which made malt whisky. We picked up lots of jugs with names we had never heard of. Having relations in the United Kingdom also helped to expand our collection. My sister became a jug packing expert and sent several by mail without a single break.

As our collection has grown I have added shelf after shelf to display them. We now have 337 jugs, each with its own story. It is a great hobby and we wish anyone starting out the best of luck and happy collecting.

Les and Peggy Musgrave, Perth, Australia

... My vintage car

Some twenty years ago I was preparing to restore a vintage car when a spirit merchant gave me a promotional "Queen Anne Scotch Whisky" drink set. The set included a water jug, ash tray, drink tray and coasters. Soon after I spotted another scotch whisky water jug of a different brand at a flea market and in no time had collected about twenty modern jugs.

In 1982 I attended the National Bottle Show which was held on the Redcliffe Peninsula at Scarborough. There I met many interesting people who all seemed to belong to a circle of addicted whisky jug collectors. From there I became involved with the Queensland Historical Bottle Club. Over a period of about fifteen years I held a number of offices including club president and vice president.

After many years collecting modern whisky jugs I got "the bug" and began to pursue older and much more expensive quality items. I have now put together a good collection of coloured and plain glass decanters, advertising mirrors, signs and other nick knacks which now make up a large part of my collection.

I am often asked which is the favourite item in my collection and like most collectors I find it hard to decide. If I was forced to make that decision I would probably say my "Perkins XXX" jug featuring a character in seventeenth century costume. I understand this jug was produced prior to World War I. With many years of collecting behind me I would have to say this has been a period of complete pleasure. I have heard collectors given the title "addict" but I prefer "devoted".

I get great pleasure from showing my collection at yearly events in Brisbane and provincial areas and look forward to meeting people, some of whom travel great distances for the same reason. However, twenty years after I started I must give some thought to what I am going to do about restoring my vintage car!

Bruce Slade, Brisbane, Australia

Keep one step ahead ...

The Australiana and Collectables catalogue/magazine offers a unique way to buy or simply keep up with market prices.

The catalogues/magazines include a photograph and detailed description of each item offered for auction as well as the anticipated price range.

"It's a fair system, no one is disadvantaged by distance and everyone has the opportunity to successfully purchase," auction co-ordinator David Westcott said.

Auctions are now conducted every two months and have been held on a similar basis for many years.

People subscribe to keep up to date with realised prices, purchase an item or two and keep up with prices being paid for similar items which they own.

David has recently completed an appraisal, for The National Museum of Australia, of a collection under consideration for their purchase.

David's knowledge and appreciation of Antiques and Collectables is evident in the detailed descriptions accompanying the photographs in the magazines.

For further information on the auction system or the catalogues themselves, you can phone:

(03) 5881 2200

or international

0011 613 5881 2200

"The Ole Bottleman!"

Gordon Litherland's name has been synonymous with whisky and ale advertising in the UK since the early 1970s. To many he is affectionately referred to as the "Ole Bottleman," an endearment which has stuck with him since 1973. While on holidays in Devon that year he found an early Victorian rubbish tip at the bottom of the garden of a three hundred year old cottage where he was staying.

His influence on bottle collecting and subsequently jug collecting in the UK is beyond compare.

In 1975 he launched a glossy magazine titled "Old Bottles and Treasure Hunting" which became the forerunner to "Antique Bottle Collecting." This new magazine focussed on items which are today eagerly sought by "Whiskiana" and "Breweriana" collectors.

Shortly after he wrote and published the first "British Bottle Price Guide" and during that same year he began a long and friendly relationship with many American collectors when he became the first British dealer to regularly exhibit at their annual National bottle fairs.

Since then he has travelled extensively throughout Europe and America in his quest to meet collectors and acquire interesting stock for his business.

Gordon has pursued his passion for almost thirty years. He is recognised as an authority in the United Kingdom and is widely respected. His International mail-order business specialises in water jugs and related advertising.

He is photographed here in September, 1999 after a successful buying trip to Scotland where he attended the closing down sale of Buchan's Thistle Pottery. Many of the stoneware jugs and decanters he acquired at this sale are unique samples or overs from "short-run" orders which were produced by Buchan's at Crieff since 1972.

Collectors travelling through England are welcome to visit Gordon. His address is:

25 Stapenhill Road, Burton-On-Trent, Staffordshire DE 15 9AE.

Burns
COTTAGE
Grant's
Deluxe Scotch
Glenfiddich
Glen Garry
FINEST
Scotch Whisky
BUCHAN
PORTOBELLO
SCOTLAND
LEGACY
21
Dewar's
FINEST
SCOTCH WHISKY
Dewar's
JAMESON
Dewar's

Buchans Portobello

The founder, Alexander Willison Buchan (1833-1904)

A.W. Buchan, Potters, Portobello.
A Short History

Location

Portobello lies some three miles east of Waverley railway station close to the sea in Edinburgh, Scotland. It is situated on a basin of clay and was consequently surrounded by a number of brick-and-tile works needed to supply the sudden increase in the building trade during the second half of the eighteenth century.

The A.W. Buchan period

Alexander Willison Buchan was born in 1833, son of a Midlothian farmer William Buchan who had married a Miss Willison five years earlier. Alexander began his career as a representative for a firm of whisky merchants and at the age of 34 acquired the Portobello pottery from Thomas Tough & Co., in 1867. Soon after he went into partnership with Thomas Murray and together they invested £1500 expanding the business. By 1872 the Murray & Buchan partnership employed 45 people.

The variety of containers which they produced continued to increase and their range now covered a variety of items including stoneware demijohns in all sizes, round & square ink bottles, foot warmers and other hot water bottles, champagne pints and quarts, jam jars, their primary product ginger beer bottles, were being produced at the rate of 2200 per day.

The 1881 census reveals that Alexander and his 45 year old wife Hester had five sons and three daughters. As well as being recognised as a "Master Potter," Alexander was also a respected magistrate. During that year their business turned over £5000.

Alexander Buchan bought out Thomas Murray and in 1890 his eldest son Samuel joined the company. In that year they were successful in winning two gold medals at the Edinburgh exhibition of pottery and glass. Their enterprise continued to prosper and although it is unclear when Mr. Buchan retired he is credited with being the driving force behind this flourishing firm.

In the latter years of the nineteenth century Samuel's younger brother Carl became a partner and plans were made for new buildings at the pottery. Fortunately a display card depicting the range of wares which Buchan's produced in 1900 has survived and is featured overleaf. Predominant in this diagram are drawings of whisky flagons and water jugs. The "Sandersons Whisky" bottle is prominent and an actual photograph is featured in this article.

Entries in the local post office directories indicate that the founder Alexander Buchan died in 1904 aged 71. This ended an outstanding era in the history of not only Buchan's but also Scottish pottery manufacture.

The Twentieth Century

In 1911 Buchan's received long term contracts with Bovril Limited for the supply of Virol jars. The arrangement was that the pottery maintain a stock of some five hundred gross (72,000) jars! After the First World War Samuel Buchan's only son Eric joined the business.

The company survived the great depression which caused the closure of so many potters in Scotland by 1930 but it was the increase in the use of glass that led to the reduction in orders for Buchan's stoneware. Shops began to give cash for returnable glass bottles used in the soft drink industry and some customers commented that they liked to see what they were buying.

Another World War had its effect on the employees at the pottery. However, the firm survived that too. Good management is reflected in the fact that the company still retained a workforce of 45 people in 1942 even though a huge fire had destroyed some of the pottery's buildings. The founder's son Samuel died in that same year.

In 1945 it was realised that the business could no longer survive on a limited range of products. Even the stoneware hot water bottles had been replaced with rubber ones. In 1949 the pottery trade throughout Britain welcomed the end to the ban on decorative wares and Buchan's began producing art pottery which had become so popular in Europe.

The coronation of Queen Elizabeth in 1953 presented the opportunity for the production of all manner of souvenirs. However, in the end the market was flooded with mass produced pottery and Buchan's did not proceed with any of their trial pieces.

Their new range of decorative and domestic pottery was successfully marketed and the company had increased its staff to 54 by 1971.

The glass industry had taken away all the bottle trade. However, there was still a demand for whisky flagons and even in 1972 – its final year of production – the pottery was making 300 dozen flagons (3600) per week.

The original pottery closed on 29th September, 1972 and some weeks later there was an extensive fire destroying the throwing shops and drying rooms. Then for safety all remaining buildings were demolished and the chimney was "dropped".

Since 1972 the "Thistle Pottery" of A.W. Buchan has been operating at Crieff, Perthshire. Mr. Eric Buchan died in 1992 in Edinburgh aged 88 years. The new types of buildings have now mellowed into their surroundings with extensive car and coach parks. Such are the large numbers of visitors that the old pottery at the seaside town of Portobello could never have accommodated.

As at Portobello, a large portion of the production during the past twenty seven years has been that of whisky flagons and jugs.

After 132 years the pottery finally closed its operation in September, 1999.

Above: "Sandersons Fine Old Highland Scotch" Buchan, Portobello, 29cm (11½") high, circa 1900, AUS $1500-2000; US $1000-1250; £800-1000.

Below: "The Doctor - Pattisons Highland Distilleries" Buchan, Portobello, 20cm (8") high, circa 1900, AUS $400-500; US $250-325; £160-200.

Above left to right: A selection of miniature jugs produced by Buchan's Thistle Pottery, since 1972. "The Culloden Old Highland Malt Whisky" "Finlaggan Islay Single Malt" "Scottish Island Malt Whisky" and "King of Scots Blended Scotch Whisky" 8cm (3¼″) high, each valued at AUS $90-110; US $50-60; £25-30.

Below left: "Bowmore Islay Single Malt Scotch Whisky" bottle, Buchan's Thistle Pottery, 30cm (12″), AUS $100-120; US $60-70; £35-40.

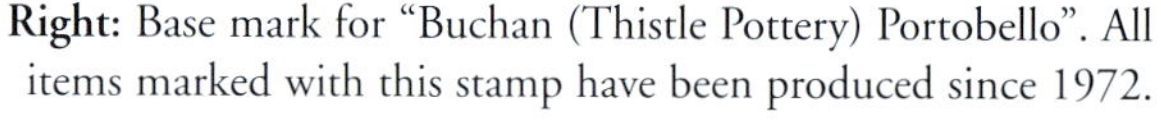
Right: Base mark for "Buchan (Thistle Pottery) Portobello". All items marked with this stamp have been produced since 1972.

Below centre: "Bulloch Lade Old Rarity De Luxe Scotch Whisky" stoneware bottle in the shape of a Victorian footwarmer. Produced at Buchan's Thistle Pottery since 1972, 12.5cm (5″) high, AUS $80-100; US $50-60; £30-35.

Below right: "Bowmore Islay Single Malt Scotch Whisky" Buchan's Thistle Pottery, 20cm (8″), AUS $200-250; US $130-160; £80-100.

A display board showing the range of stoneware products together with catalogue numbers which Buchans produced in 1900. In 1869 Buchans were producing more than 12,000 store ginger beer bottles, 1,700 large cylindrical ink botttles and hundreds of miscellaneous items every week. A colour photograph of the board can be viewed in the Crieff Visitor Centre.

About This Guide

Above: "White Horse Whisky" Made in England, (Shelley), 14cm (5½"), AUS $400-500; US $250-300; £160-180.

In an effort to improve on the past, and with collectors in mind, we have enhanced this publication in a few subtle ways.

One of the improvements is the move to full colour photographs of each and every item included. This is an attempt to make identifying the huge variety of contents easier and at the same time add to the appeal and legibility of the book.

Another innovation can be found in the index where simple codes have been added to help direct readers to their items of interest.

You can now look up Ainslie's, for example, and at a glance see which pages include bar figures, ashtrays or other non-jug items. The legend appears at the bottom of each index page for easy reference and we trust it will help you to locate your "special item" quickly and easily.

Below: "Stewart's Dundee Cream Of The Barley" tin serving tray, 35cm (13½") square, AUS $45-55; US $25-30; £15-20.

Below: "John Dewar & Sons" match-striker, Doulton Lambeth, 8 x 8.5cm (3¼ x 3½"), AUS $500-600; US $300-350; £200-220.

In addition we have included metric and imperial measurements to assist collectors worldwide regardless of their country's measuring system.

Lastly and perhaps most importantly all items are valued in Australian dollars, US dollars and UK pounds sterling.

Indexing example:

at - **Ash Tray** ca - **calendar**

bf - **Bar Figure** j - **Jug**

bt - **Bar Tray** ms - **match-striker**

White Horse *Whisky* j, 26
Stewart's *Dundee* bt, 26
Dewar's John & Sons ms, 26
Johnnie Walker *Scotch Whisky* ca, 27
King George IV *Top Notch* at, 27
Robbie Burns *Scotch Whisky* bf, 27

Right: "Robbie Burns Famed Old Scotch Whisky" rubber compound figure, 32cm (12½") high, AUS $800-1000; US $500-600; £300-350.

Below: "Johnnie Walker Scotch Whisky" tin calendar, 24 x 23cm (9½ x 9"), AUS $140-170; US $90-110; £55-65.

Below: "King George IV Top Notch Scotch Whisky" ashtray, base marked with Reg. No. 599183, 13cm (5") wide, AUS $220-250; US $130-160; £85-100.

Ainslie's

Ainslie and Heilbron Distillers of Glasgow is the product of countless mergers and takeovers spanning a 130 year history.

The origins of the distillery have been traced back to 1868 when wine and spirit merchants James Ainslie and Co began operation. In 1896 they took over the Clynelish Distillery and two years later completely rebuilt it. Soon after they suffered a change of fortune but avoided bankruptcy until 1912 when partners Distillers Company Limited and John Risk combined to form the Clynelish Distillery Company Limited. In 1913 James Ainslie and Co amalgamated with Walter Baillie and Sons, Robertson Brothers and John Gillon and Co to form Ainslie, Baillie and Co Ltd of Leith.

When the company was liquidated in 1921 by the son of the original James Ainslie it passed into the hands of Sir James Calder who had acquired another firm of whisky merchants David Heilbron and Son.

The two companies merged with Colville Greenlees to become Ainslie and Heilbron (Distillers) Ltd and in 1922 relocated their operations to Glasgow where they have traded since.

Ainslie and Heilbron (Distillers) Ltd became part of the DCL empire when the firm incorporating Greenlees was sold.

Below: Rare green and white version of the jug advertising "Ainslie's Scotch as supplied to the Royal Navy." It features a First World War submarine with a bottle of Ainslie's on the bow, titled "Ainslie's has risen to the top" base stamped "Royal Doulton" circa 1919, 12cm (4¾″), AUS $3500-4000; US $2000-2500; £1500-1750.

Left: "Ainslie's Whisky" no base mark, 18.5cm (7″), AUS $400-500; US $250-300; £150-200.

Right: "Ainslie's Scotch Whiskies" no base mark, 11cm (4″), AUS $250-300; US $150-200; £100-125.

"Ainslie's Whisky" no base mark, 13cm (5¼"), AUS $200-250; US $125-150, £75-100.

"Anchor Blend Scotch Whisky" Wade Regicor, 10cm (4"), AUS $200-250; US $125-150; £75-100.

"The Antiquary" Wade Regicor, 12cm (4¾"), AUS $200-250; US $125-150; £75-100.

"Ainslie's Scotch Whiskies" no base mark, 13cm (5¼"), AUS $90-120; US $60-80; £35-45.

"Ainslie's Whisky" ashbowl, Causton London, 11cm (4½"), AUS $200-250; US $125-150; £75-100.

A Round "Ainslie's Whisky" change tray, Causton London, 14cm (5½") dia, AUS $100-120; US $60-75; £40-50.

Above: "Ainslie's King's Legend Scotch Whisky" HCW, 13cm (5¼"), AUS $200-250; US $125-150; £75-100.

Below: "Ainslie's King's Legend" Grays Pottery, 12cm (4¾"), AUS $225-300; US $140-170; £90-120.

Below: "Ainslie's King's Legend" tray, 42 x 32cm (16½" x 13"), AUS $200-250; US $125-150; £75-100.

Above: "Archer's Light Scotch Whisky" Piola, 11.5cm (4½″), AUS $90-110; US $55-65; £35-45.

Above: "Angus McKay" Piola, 18cm (7″), AUS $85-95; US $50-60; £30-35.

Above: Aberlour" HCW, 14.5cm (5¾″), AUS $85-95; US $50-60; £30-35.

Right: "The Antiquary Old Scotch Whisky" match-holder, Wedekind & Co., London, 7.5cm (3″), AUS $200-250; US $125-150; £75-85.

Left: "Ainslie's Whiskies" matchstriker, 11.5cm (4½″), AUS $175-200; US $110-130; £70-90.

Below left: "Allsopp's Ales" no base mark,17.5cm (6¾″), AUS $1500-2000; US $1000-1250; £650-750.

Below right: "Allsopp's" (Ales) change tray, Royal Doulton, 16cm (6¼″), AUS $400-500; US $250-300; £150-175.

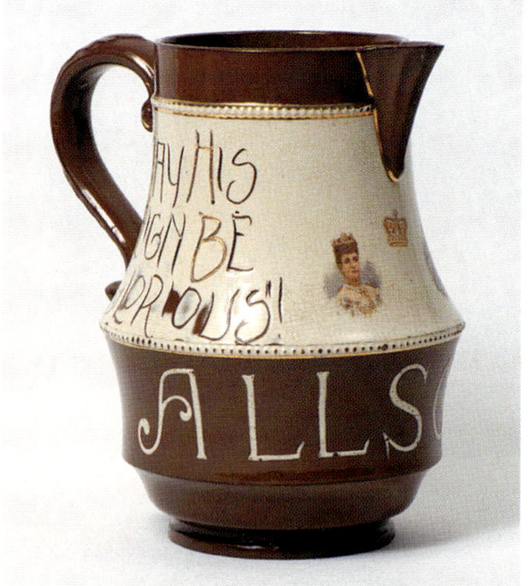

"Ainslie's Whisky" Causton London, 17cm (6¾") high, AUS $300-350; US $200-230; £120-140.

"Antiquary" Euroceramics, 14cm (5½"), AUS $80-90; US $50-60; £30-35.

"The Antiquary De Luxe Old Scotch Whisky" Barcelona, 17.5cm (7"), AUS $80-100; US $50-60; £30-35.

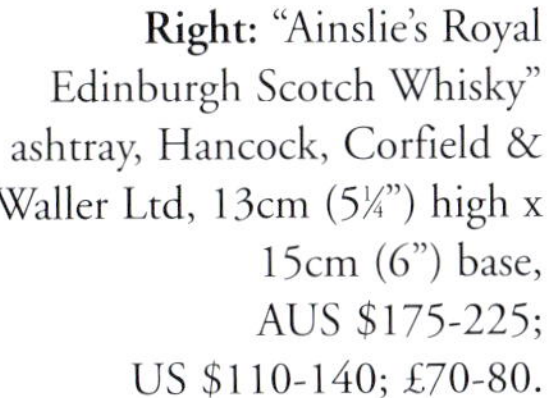

Right: "Ainslie's Royal Edinburgh Scotch Whisky" ashtray, Hancock, Corfield & Waller Ltd, 13cm (5¼") high x 15cm (6") base, AUS $175-225; US $110-140; £70-80.

"The Abbot's Choice Scotch Whisky" rubber compound figure, 17cm (6¾"), AUS $600-700; US $350-400; £200-250.

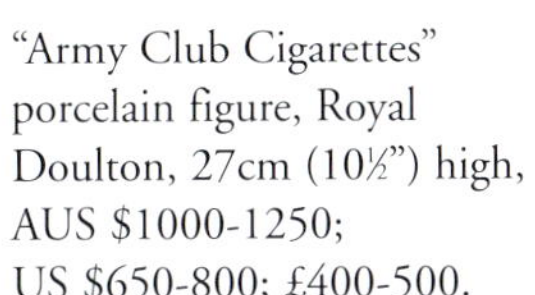

"Army Club Cigarettes" porcelain figure, Royal Doulton, 27cm (10½") high, AUS $1000-1250; US $650-800; £400-500.

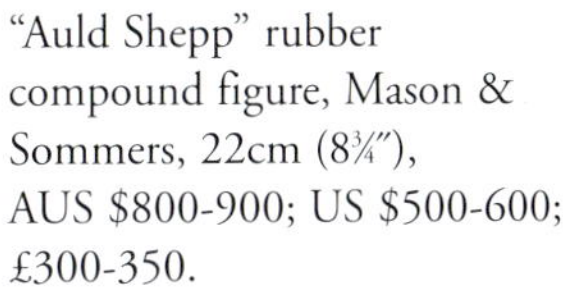

"Auld Shepp" rubber compound figure, Mason & Sommers, 22cm (8¾"), AUS $800-900; US $500-600; £300-350.

"Auchentoshan Single Malt Scotch Whisky" Buchan Portobello, 16cm (6¼"), AUS $110-130; US $70-80; £40-50.

"Ancient Clan Blended Scotch Whisky" Bristile Fine China, Australia, 13cm (5"), AUS $80-100; US $60-70; £35-40.

"Apollinaris" no base mark, 10cm (4"), AUS $200-250; US $125-150; £75-85.

Above left: "Atkinson's Aston Ales" Upton & Sons England, 10.5cm (4¼"), AUS $700-800; US $450-550; £275-325. **Above right:** "Atkinson's Aston Ales" Shelley, 12cm (4¾"), AUS $800-1000, US $500-600; £300-400.

"Ballantine's Scotch Whisky" Piola, 14cm (5½"), AUS $60-75; US $40-50; £20-25.

"Ballantine's Scotch Whisky" Piola, 12cm (4¾"), AUS $55-65; US $35-40; £20-25.

"Ballantine's Scotch Whisky" Piola, 15cm (6"), AUS $60-75; US $40-50; £20-25

"Bailie Nicol Jarvie Scotch Whisky" James Green & Nephew, 11.5cm (4½″), AUS $350-400; US $225-250; £140-165.

"Ballantine's Scotch Whisky" Wade Regicor, 10cm (4″), AUS $175-225; US $110-130; £65-75.

"Bailie Nicol Jarvie" Made in England, 13cm (5¼″), AUS $550-650; US $350-400; £220-250.

"Beneagles Scotch Whisky" Made in England, 12cm (4¾″), AUS $200-250; US $130-160; £80-100.

"John Begg" Wade Regicor, 13cm (5¼″), AUS $125-150; US $80-90; £50-60.

"Benmore Scotch Whisky" Globe, Great Britain, 10cm (4″), AUS $175-200; US $110-130; £70-80.

Below: Both sides and front view of the "Barnsley Brewery" jug. The artwork which Royal Doulton created for this jug is generally regarded as their finest on any advertising jug which they produced. This magnificent jug actually advertises three different companies: "Brown Corbett & Co. Irish Whiskey" "Barnsley Brewery Co. Ltd. Famous Mild and Bitter Ales, Oakwell" and "Edward Young & Co. K.L. Scotch Whisky, Liverpool and Glasgow" 16cm (6¼″) high, AUS $3000-3500; US $1750-2000; £1000-1250

Left"Bell's" "Afore ye go" Thorne's Adv. Services, 11cm (4½″), AUS $400-450; US $250-300; £160-185.

Right"Bell's" "Afore ye go" Causton London, 12cm (4¾″), AUS $350-400; US $225-250; £130-160.

Above left: "Bell's Finest Scotch Whisky" Elischer Aust., 15.5cm (6″), AUS $400-500; US $250-300; £150-175. **Above centre:** "Bell's Extra Special" Elischer Aust., 13cm (5″), AUS $400-500; US $250-300; £150-175. **Above right:** "Bell's Extra Special" Elischer Aust., 15.5cm (6″), AUS $400-500; US $250-300; £150-175.

Below left: "Bell's" Elischer Aust., 28.5cm (11¼″), AUS $200-250; US $130-160; £80-100.
Below centre: "Bell's" Elischer Aust., 16.5cm (6½″), AUS $200-250; US $130-160; £80-100.
Below right: "Bell's" Elischer Aust., 18.5cm (7¼″), AUS $300-350; US $200-250; £120-150.

"Bell's" "Afore ye go" Associated Pottery, 10cm (4″), AUS $450-500; US $300-350; £175-225.

"Bell's Finest Old Scotch Whisky" Wade, 15.5cm (6″), AUS $70-85; US $45-60; £25-30.

"Bell's" Tilstone Ware, 14cm (5½″), AUS $100-120; US $65-75; £40-50.

"Blair Athol Malt Scotch Whisky" Piola, 11.5cm (4½″), AUS $55-65; US $30-40; £20-25.

Miniature "Bowmore Islay Single Malt Scotch Whisky" no base mark, 5.5cm (2¼″), AUS $70-90; US $45-55; £25-30.

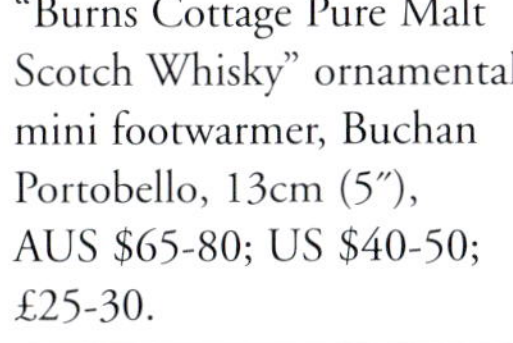

"Burns Cottage Pure Malt Scotch Whisky" ornamental mini footwarmer, Buchan Portobello, 13cm (5″), AUS $65-80; US $40-50; £25-30.

"Bowmore Islay Scotch Whisky" Buchan Portobello, 14cm (5½″), AUS $80-100; US $50-65; £30-35.

"Burns Cottage Pure Malt Scotch Whisky" Buchan Portobello, 9cm (3½″), AUS $150-200; US $100-120; £60-75.

"John Brown & Co Imperial Scotch Whisky" matchstriker, Wedekind & Co. London, 11cm (4½″), AUS $150-170; US $100-120; £60-75.

Buchanan's

Buchanan's Black and White Scotch Whisky label is arguably one of the best known in the world. The blend behind the label had its origins in London where James Buchanan first set up business on his own in 1879. With some experience as an agent for Leith based whisky blenders Mackinlay and Co, Buchanan arranged financial backing from a friend and was soon taking orders from the London cigar and wine merchants Dolomore Ltd.

Buchanan began trading by the barrel but soon recognised the potential for bottled whisky and set about perfecting a blend to suit for the English palate.

Some of London's most prestigious hotels and restaurants soon carried the Buchanan blend along with the Member's Bar at the House of Commons and the London music halls.

The blend went through a series of name changes before settling on the "Black and White" label, a title registered in 1904.

The years between 1890 and 1914 saw Buchanan's business prosper and develop. Royal orders for Black and White along with the Red Seal label came repeatedly from King Edward VII and from the Prince of Wales.

The popularity of the product in England spurred Buchanan on to similar successes in Germany, Canada, the USA, New Zealand and South Africa.

Quality, salesmanship and a head for business stood Buchanan in good stead. He recognised the need to handle his product from start to finish and in 1898 built his own "state of the art" malt distillery. He later acquired two more distilleries.

The Black and White label went hand in hand with quality and innovative marketing ensured Buchanan's ongoing success. He was among the first whisky makers to use newspaper advertising and his delivery vans, complete with immaculately groomed horses, were distinctive on the streets of London.

Early this century, with the whisky industry in turmoil, Buchanan's and Dewar's joined forces in a bid to rival the stranglehold of DCL. In 1922 the partnership had acquired or held interests in eleven distilleries but further expansion was to come before

Left: "Buchanan's Special Red Seal" Frank Beardmore & Co Fenton, 20cm (8″), AUS $3000-3500; US $2000-2500; £1250-1500.

Above left: "Buchanan's Special Red Seal" Frank Beardmore & Co Fenton, 20cm (8″), AUS $3000-3500; US $2000-2500; £1250-1500. **Above centre:** "Buchanan's Special Red Seal" Frank Beardmore & Co Fenton, 20cm (8″), AUS $3000-3500; US $2000-2500; £1250-1500. **Above right:** One of the rarest in this series "Buchanan's Special Red Seal" Frank Beardmore & Co Fenton, 20cm (8″), AUS $4500-5000, US $3000-3500; £2000-2500.

Below left: "Buchanan's Special Red Seal" Frank Beardmore & Co Fenton, titled "The Rivals" signed by artist Victor Venner, 20cm (8″), AUS $3000-3500; US $2000-2500; £1250-1500. **Below centre:** One of the rarest in this series "Buchanan's Special Red Seal" Frank Beardmore & Co Fenton, titled "Legal Advice" signed by artist Victor Venner, 20cm (8"), AUS $4500-5000; US $3000-3500; £2000-2500. **Below right**: "Buchanan's Special Red Seal" Frank Beardmore & Co Fenton, titled "Tale of the Hunt" signed by artist Victor Venner, 20cm (8″), AUS $3000-3500, US $2000-2500; £1250-1500.

the amalgamation of DCL and Buchanan-Dewar Ltd in 1925.

Despite the amalgamation Buchanan's was able to retain its identity.

In 1926 when the general strike threatened to paralyse all business in England, Buchanan embarked on an ambitious expansion of his business in Australia where his whisky had always sold well. The move was a blessing in disguise because the site he chose to expand his business increased dramatically in value when the Sydney Harbour bridge was built in 1932.

Buchanan's achievements were honoured with the title of Baronet in 1920 and much later, at the age of 70 with a knighthood.

Buchanan's Special (Red Seal)

By far the rarest of the "Buchanan's Special Red Seal" jugs, this example features an unusual transfer printed turkey scene, 20cm (8″) high, base stamped "Frank Beardmore & Co., Fenton" AUS $7000 10,000; US $4500-6500; £3000-4000.

Above: Full deck of playing cards advertising "Black & White Scotch Whisky" featuring two greyhounds AUS $200-250; US $150-200; £80-100.

Below: Full deck of playing cards advertising "Black & White Scotch Whisky" featuring dogs playing and titled "Best of Spirits" AUS $150-200; US $100-125; £60-70.

Above: "Black & White Scotch Whisky" bridge book of rules, 20 x 10cm (8 x 4″) high, AUS $80-100; US $50-65; £30-40.

Above: "Buchanan's Black & White Whisky" metal figure, 26cm (10¼″), AUS $500-700; US $325-400; £200-250.

Below: "Black & White Scotch Whisky" porcelain clock, no potter's stamp, 22.5cm (9″) high, latest Australian auction price AUS $200-250; US $100-125; £45-65.

Below: "Black & White" figure with racing car flags and bottle, 14cm (5½″), AUS $600-800; US $400-450; £250-300.

Below right: "James Buchanan & Co." fob chain note book, 7 x 4.5cm (2¾″ x 1¾″), AUS $75-100; US $50-65; £30-40.

Above: "Buchanan's Black & White Scotch Whisky" plastic cigarette dispenser, 28cm (11″), AUS $120-150; US 75-100; £50-65.

Below: "Black & White Scotch" US distillers base stamp, 17cm (6¾″), AUS $130-160; US $75-100; £50-65.

Above: "Black & White Scotch Whisky" Brentleigh Ware figure, 24cm (9½″) with a 750ml bottle of "Black & White Scotch Whisky" AUS $300-350; US $185-225; £120-140.

Below: "Black & White Scotch Whisky" plaster figure, bottle in centre, 30cm (15¾″) high to tip of dog's ears, AUS $450-650; US 300-330; £175-200.

Above left: "Black & White Scotch Whisky" ashbowl, James Green & Nephew, 12cm (4¾") dia, AUS $100-130; US $65-85; £40-50. **Above right:** "Black & White Scotch Whisky" nickel plated menu holder, 7cm (2¾") high, AUS $200-250; US $130-160; £80-100.

Right: Rare rubber compound figure "Buchanan's Black & White Scotch Whisky - Something to crow about" 30cm (12") high, AUS $2000-2500; US $1300-1600; £800-1000.

Below: Glass decanter "Black & White Scotch Whisky" 27cm (10½"), AUS $300-350; US $200-225; £120-150.

Rajah's Pride:

This advertising piece was brought to Australia from India relatively recently. It has the same dimensions (height, diameter, etc.) as a normal bottle of Black & White whisky. It is of solid silver construction - i.e. it is not silver plated. The silver is of the same thickness as the glass would be in a similar bottle.

Similarly, the centre of the bottle is hollow in the same way as a glass bottle would be hollow to permit it to accommodate its contents.

It has undoubtedly been made in India – the silver and the silver-work are unmistakably Indian. It was most likely made in the period 1905-1910. It is reasonable to assume that it was a piece which Buchanan's specially commissioned as a presentation piece for a member of the Indian nobility (possibly one of the Maharajas) or as a centrepiece for the bar or dining room for senior officers of one of the English or Scottish regiments stationed in India in that era.

There is little doubt that is was the only example of that type ever made – i.e. it was a "one off" piece which is truly unique in every sense of the expression.

Right: "Black & White" Silver Bottle, 30cm (12″) high, AUS $2000-2500; US $1300-1600; £800-1000.

"Buchanan's Whisky" match-striker, R. Hammersly & Son Burslem, 9cm (3½"), AUS $800-1000, US $500-650, £300-375.

"Buchanan Old Original" ashbowl, Empire Ware, Stoke-On-Trent, 12cm (4¾"), AUS $200-250; US $125-150; £80-100.

"Buchanan's Black & White Whisky" matchbox holder, Shelley, 9cm (3½"), AUS $600-750; US $400-450; £250-300.

Left: "Buchanan's Scotch Whiskies" Made In England, 18cm (7"), AUS $80-100; US $50-65; £20-25.

Above: "Black & White Scotch" rubber compound figure, 15cm to top of dogs (6"), AUS $500-650; US $325-375; £200-250.

Left: "Black & White" tray, entitled "Honest Friends" 30cm (15¾") dia, AUS $500-650, US $300-350; £200-250.

New Release

Above: Recent series of "Black & White" jugs numbered 1-9, on base. Made in Staffordshire, England, 12.5cm (5″), latest Australian auction prices vary from AUS $125-150; US $50-70; £25-35 each.

Above left: Tin serving tray advertising "Buchanan's Black & White Scotch Whisky" featuring an eagle with prey, 40 x 30cm (16 x 12″), AUS $600-700; US $400-500; £250-300. **Above right:** Oval tin serving tray advertising "Jas Buchanan & Co. Ltd. Scotch Whisky Distillers" featuring a polo player, 42 x 34cm (16½ x 13½″), AUS $500-600; US $300-350; £200-250.

Below left: Tin calendar advertising "Black & White Scotch Whisky" entitled "Honest Friends" 33 x 23cm (13 x 9″) high, AUS $800-1000; US $500-600; £300-400. **Below right:** Framed cardboard display card advertising "Buchanan's Black & White Scotch Whisky" featuring a horse drawn wagon full of cases of this whisky, 63cm (25") high, AUS $900-1200; US $600-750; £350-500.

Rectangular tin calendar advertising "Black & White Scotch Whisky" featuring the two terriers running down the stairs to welcome their master, entitled "My Never Failing Friends" 33 x 23cm (13 x 9"), AUS $800-1000; US $500-600; £300-400.

Above: Framed off-white ceramic battery operated clocks advertising "Black & White (Scotch Whisky) - "The secret is in the blending" and "The pick of them all" 35 x 28cm (14″ x 11"), recently produced, latest Australian auction price AUS $150-200; US $100-125; £50-65

Right: Enamelled jug "Jas Buchanan & Co. Ltd. Black & White Whisky" 15cm (6″), AUS $500-650; US $325-350; £200-225.

Next page: Recent series of eight jugs advertising "Black & White" Scotch Whisky titled as follows:

(1) Right at any time

(2) The pick of them all

(3) Sure of a good welcome

(4) With a view to good entertainment

(5) The secret is in the blending

(6) It speaks volumes for your good taste

(7) Nelson's column

(8) Only the best in this house

Bases numbered 1-8 and stamped "Made In England" 13cm (5″) high, latest Australian auction price AUS $125-150; US $45-55; £20-25.

Right at
any time
'BLACK
&
WHITE'
The Secret is in the Blending
1

The pick
of them all
Why do connoisseurs of Scotch Whisky name "Black & White" first? Because they know the special way "Black & White" is blended gives it a flavour and character all its own.
'BLACK
&
WHITE'
The Secret is in the Blending
2

Sure of a
good welcome
'BLACK
&
WHITE'
SCOTCH WHISKY
3

With a view
to good
entertainment
'BLACK
&
WHITE'
The Secret is in the Blending
4

The Secret
is in the
Blending
BLACK & WHITE
'BLACK
&
WHITE'
SCOTCH WHISKY
5

It speaks volumes
for your good taste
'BLACK
&
WHITE'
The Secret is in the Blending
6

"Nelson from his column
keeps a look-out over
all London,"
"And all-London
keeps a look-out
for 'Black & White'."
'BLACK
&
WHITE'
SCOTCH WHISKY
7

Only the best
in this house
'BLACK
&
WHITE'
SCOTCH WHISKY
8

Left: "Buchanan's Black & White" ashbowl, Shelley, 5.5cm (2″) high, AUS $400-450; US $250-300; £150-180.
Right: "Black & White" ashbowl, Shelley, 5.5cm (2″), AUS $250-300; US $150-200; £100-130.

Left: "Black & White Scotch Whisky" ashtray, Made in England, 12.5cm (4¾″), AUS $140-180; US $90-120; £55-65.
Right: "Black & White Scotch Whisky" ashtray, James Green & Nephew, 13cm (5″), AUS $75-100; US $50-65; £30-40

Left: "Black & White Scotch Whisky" ashtray, Made In England, 12.5cm (4¾″), AUS $150-200; US $100-130; £60-80.
Right: "Black & White Scotch Whisky" ashtray, Shelley, 12.5cm (4¾″), AUS $400-500; US $250-300; £170-200.

Left: "Black & White Scotch Whisky" ashtray, Shelley, 12.5cm (4¾″), AUS $175-225; US $110-140; £70-90.
Right: "Buchanan's Black & White" ashtray, Shelley, 12.5cm (4¾″), AUS $200-250; US $130-160; £80-100.

Above: "Buchanan's 8 Years Old" Scandia, 13cm (5¼"), AUS $150-200; US $100-130; £60-80.

Above: Tin serving tray advertising "Black & White Scotch Whisky" featuring cattle grazing, 30cm (15¾") dia, AUS $600-800; US $400-500; £250-300.

Above: "Black & White Is The Scotch" no base mark, 11cm (4½"), AUS $80-100; US $50-65; £30-40.

Below: Matching jug & ashtray advertising "Buchanan's Black & White Scotch Whisky" jug base stamped Made In England, 12.5cm (4¾"), AUS $600-700; US $375-450; £240-280. The ashtray is base stamped Shelley, 12.5cm (4¾"), AUS $200-250; US $130-160; £80-100.

Left: "Drambuie Bonnie Prince Charlie" rubber compound figure, 33cm (13″), AUS $400-500; US $275-325; £150-200.

Above: "Bulloch Lade" Made in England, 11.5cm (4½″), AUS $1200-1500; US $800-1000; £500-650.

Below left: "Burke's Three Star Dublin Whisky" Fielding, 17cm (6¾″), AUS $800-1000; US $500-650; £300-400. **Below right:** "Burke's Green Label Whisky" toby jug, Fielding, 29cm (11¼″), AUS $2000-2500; US $1250-1500; £800-1000.

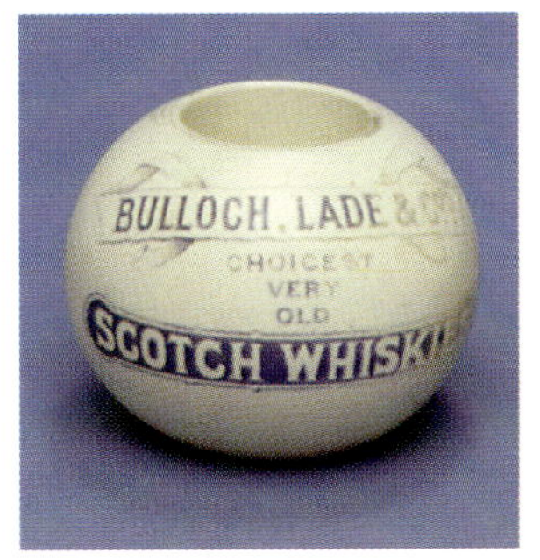

Above left: "Bulloch Lade Old Rarity De Luxe Scotch Whisky" Buchan Portobello, 12.5cm (5″), latest Australian auction price AUS $150-180; US $100-125; £60-80.

Above centre: "Bulloch Lade Blended Scotch Whisky" ashtray, West Highland Pottery Co., 11.5cm (4½″) dia, AUS $50-65; US $30-40; £20-25.

Above right: "Bulloch Lade Scotch Whisky" matchstriker, Stewart & Woolf, London, 12.5cm (5″) dia, AUS $140-165; US $90-120; £50-65.

Right: "Bulloch Lade & Co's Choicest Very Old Scotch Whisky" match-holder, no base stamp, 7cm (2¾″), AUS $150-175; US $100-130; £60-75.

Below: "Corbett's Irish Whisky" toby jug, Rd. No. 628478, 20cm (8″), AUS $1200-1500; US $750-900; £500-600.

Below: "Cobbold's Lancer Whisky, Ipswich" no base stamp, 14.5cm (6″), AUS $1000-1250; US $650-800; £400-500.

Above: "Catto's The Sportsman - Scotch Whisky" porcelain figure, 30cm (11¾"), AUS $600-800; US $400-500; £250-325.

Above: "Cobbold's Special Cardinal Whiskies" Fielding, 15cm (6"), AUS $2500-3000; US $1500-1800; £1000-1300.

Above: "Captain Morgan Rum" rubber compound figure, 32cm (12¾"), AUS $500-700; US $325-375; £200-250.

Above: "The Cabinet Whisky" Doulton Lambeth, 17cm (6¾"), AUS $800-1000; US $500-650; £300-375.

Below: "Curries No. 10 Perth Whisky" rubber compound figure, 10.5cm (4¼"), AUS $1250-1500; US $800-1000; £500-650.

Below: "The Challenge Whiskey" Port Dundas, 16cm (6¼"), AUS $1250-1500; US $800-1000; £500-650.

Below: "Courvoisier, The Brandy Of Napolean" rubber compound figure, 32cm (12¾"), AUS $700-900; US $450-550; £200-250.

Top left: "Claymore Blended Scotch Whisky" Seton Pottery, 14cm (5½"), AUS $200-250; US $125-150; £80-100.

Above right: "Chivas Regal Blended Scotch Whisky" Wade, 12cm (4¾"), AUS $140-170; US $90-120; £55-65.

Left: "Club 99 Scotch Whisky" Euroceramics, 13cm (5"), AUS $70-90; US $45-60; £30-40.

Lower left: "Canadian Club" Wade Regicor, 16.5cm (6¼"), AUS $150-200; US $100-130; £60-80.

Below left: "Cognac Bisquit" rubber compound figure, 42cm (16¾"), AUS $900-1200; US $600-750; £350-450.

Below centre: "Cavalier Best Pale Ale" rubber compound figure, 32cm (12¾"), AUS $650-850; US $400-500; £250-325.

Right: "Clan Campbell Deluxe Blended Scotch Whisky" ceramic decanter, 36cm (14"), AUS $125-165; US $80-100; £50-65.

"Cowan's Old Irish Whisky" Campbell & Sons Belfast, circa 1910, 13.5cm (5¼"), AUS $1750-2250; US $1000-1250; £700-850.

Tin advertising sign "Cork Distilleries Co. Ltd. Whisky - Pure Pot Still" 42 x 32cm (16½ x 12½") wide, AUS $200-250; US $125-150; £80-100.

Above: "Cluny Scotch Whisky" no base mark, 17.5cm (6¾"), AUS $90-110; US $60-75; £35-45.

Above: "Crawford's Special Reserve Old Scotch Whisky" no base mark, 16.5cm (6¼"), AUS $80-100; US $50-60; £30-35.

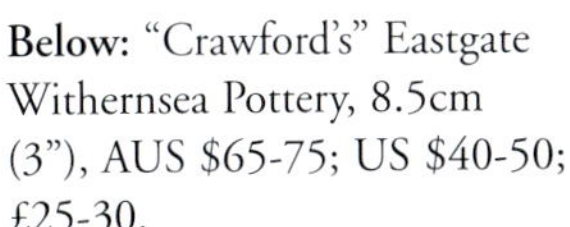

Below: "Crawford's" Eastgate Withernsea Pottery, 8.5cm (3"), AUS $65-75; US $40-50; £25-30.

Above: "Carlton Finest Scotch Whisky" Euroceramics, 12cm (4½"), AUS $70-90; US $45-55; £25-30.

Below: "Crawford's Five Star" Seton Pottery, 16.5cm (6¼"), AUS $125-150; US $80-100; £50-60.

Below: "Ask For Crawford's C.C.C., Old Scotch Whisky" Fielding & Co., 17cm (6¾"), AUS $2500-3000; US $1600-1900; £1000-1250.

Above: "Clan Campbell Blended Scotch Whisky" Euroceramics, 15cm (6"), AUS $65-85; US $40-50; £25-30.

Below: "Crawford's Special Reserve Old Scotch Whisky" no base mark, 15.5cm (6"), AUS $80-100; US $50-60; £30-35.

Below: "Crawford's" Seton Pottery, 17cm (6¾"), AUS $130-170; US $85-100; £50-60.

Cutty Sark

Cutty Sark was the first of the "light" whiskies blended especially for export by London based wine and whisky merchants Berry Brothers & Rudd Ltd.

The blend was destined for the Bahamas market, then regarded as the "back door" into prohibition America.

In a bid to avoid "tampering" with the Berry Bros blend, the firm established links with Captain Bill McCoy who ensured a steady supply of Cutty Sark into the USA during prohibition.

Cutty Sark established a reputation in the country and when the prohibition laws were finally repealed Cutty Sark sales sky rocketed.

World War II saw sales fall but the surge continued from 1945 onwards. Cutty Sark first became the top selling Scotch whisky in the USA in 1961 and since then has remained one of the leading brands on the market.

The brand owners Berry Bros and Rudd Ltd do not own a distillery but are responsible for bottling, packaging, shipping and marketing Cutty Sark abroad. The principal blend is made up by Robertson and Baxter Ltd of Glasgow.

Above left: Yellow "Cutty Sark" jug, Milano, 8cm (3"), AUS $65-75; US $40-50; £25-30.
Above centre: "Cutty Sark Scotch Whisky" ashbowl, no base stamp, 11cm (4.25) dia, AUS $35-45; US $20-25; £15-20. **Above right:** Pastel blue "Cutty Sark" jug, Milano, 8cm (3"), AUS $65-75; US $40-50; £25-30.

"Cutty Sark Scots Whisky" Amberglade, Derbyshire, jug recently produced in four different sizes:
11.5cm (4½") and 14.5cm (5¾"), AUS $80-100; US $50-60; £30-35,
17cm (6¾"), AUS $100-120; US $65-75; £40-50,
19cm (7½"), AUS $120-150; US $80-100; £50-60.

"Cutty Sark" TLH, 16.5cm (6½"), AUS $175-225; US $100-120; £70-90.

"Cutty Sark" Made In China, 11cm (4½"), AUS $90-120; US $60-70; £35-45.

"Dew Of The Highlands - Rowson & Sons, Chester" stoneware, no base mark, 8.5cm (3"), AUS $250-300; US $160-190; £100-125.

Left: "Dandie Dinmont" Wade, 10cm (4"), AUS $100-125; US $65-80; £40-50.

Right: "Dawson's" ashbowl, Causton, 4cm (1¾") high, AUS $175-225; US $110-130; £70-90.

"Peter Dawson Whisky - Pharlap" plaster figure, 30cm (11¾"), AUS $1500-2000; US $1000-1250; £650-850.

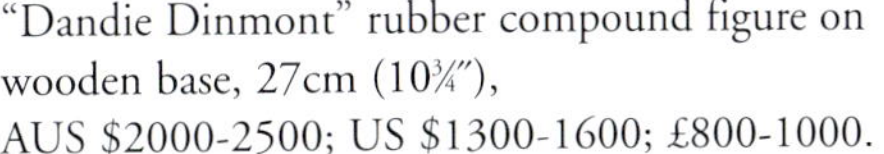
"Dandie Dinmont" rubber compound figure on wooden base, 27cm (10¾"), AUS $2000-2500; US $1300-1600; £800-1000.

Left: "Dawson's Scotch Whisky" ashbowl, Carlton Ware, AUS $120-150; US $80-100; £50-60.

Right: "D.C.L. Gold Medal Scotch Whisky" No Base Stamp, 11.5cm (4½"), AUS $350-450; US $225-275; £140-180.

Left: "Dickens Scotch Whisky" Made In England, 12cm (4¾"), AUS $350-450; US $225-265; £140-170.

Right: "Deerstakler" HCW, 10cm (4"), AUS $220-250; US $140-170; £90-120

Two ashtrays advertising "D.C.L. Scotch Whisky."
Left: Associated Potteries version, 12.5 x 9.5cm (5 x 3¾"), AUS $325-400; US $225-275; £125-150.
Right: Doulton Burslem version, 10 x 7cm (4 x 2¾"), AUS $325-400; US $225-275; £125-150.

Right: Green glass jug with clear glass handle, "Daniel Crawford Finest Very Old Scotch Whisky" 18cm (7") high, AUS $1200-1500; US $750-900; £500-650.

Below: Two scarce coloured glass jugs advertising "D.C.L. Scotch Whisky." **Left:** Green glass, 18cm (7"), AUS $1000-1250; US $650-800; £450-600.
Right: Cranberry glass, 20cm (8"), AUS $1200-1600; US $800-1000; £500-650.

Above left: "Dunville's V.R" W.J. Irvine, 9.5cm (3¾"), AUS $175-225; US $100-125; £70-85. **Above centre:** "D.C.L. Scotch Whisky" copper ashbowl, 7cm (2¾") high x 9cm (3½") dia, AUS $125-150; US $80-100; £50-65. **Above right:** "Dunville's V.R." matchstriker, Shelley, late Foley, 11.5cm (4½") dia, AUS $150-200; US $100-130; £60-80

Right: "Duff's Liqueur Scotch Whisky" Mintons Regicor, 11cm (4¼"), AUS $300-350; US $200-250; £120-160.

Below: "Peter Dawson's P.D. Scotch Whisky" aluminium jug 21cm (8¼"), AUS $120-150; US $80-100; £50-65.

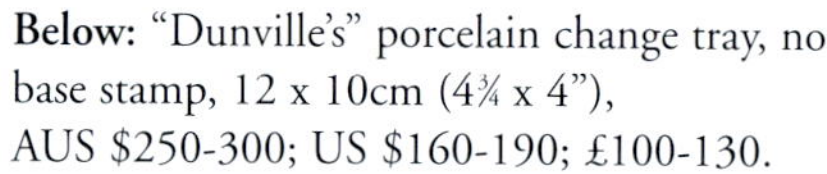

Below: "Dunville's" porcelain change tray, no base stamp, 12 x 10cm (4¾ x 4"), AUS $250-300; US $160-190; £100-130.

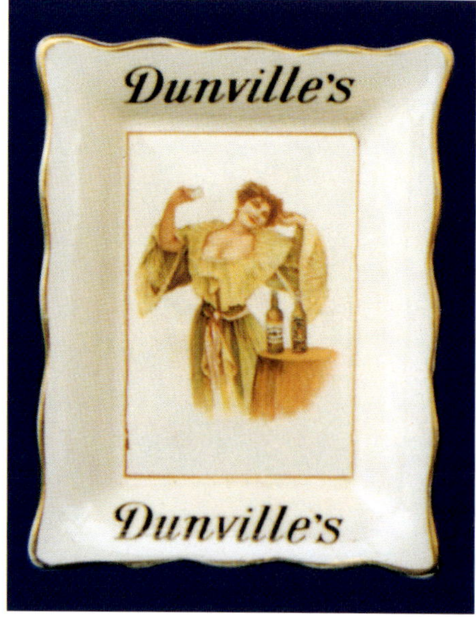

Dewar's

With each new generation of the Dewar family, John Dewar and Sons Ltd expanded its operations. From humble beginnings in Perth, Scotland, the company developed an international outlook with more than 90 percent of its total production destined for export.

The Dewar family dynasty began in 1846 when the original John Dewar established a modest whisky blending and bottling operation in Perth.

He learned the trade while working in the cellars of his distant cousin's wine merchant business. Close to the premises where he worked once lived the "Fair Maid of Perth," a title which would one day form part of a Dewar's advertising slogan.

Less than ten years after joining his cousin's business John Dewar was made a partner but in 1846 decided he could achieve more on his own and established John Dewar and Sons Ltd.

He began on a small scale but was soon looking beyond the limits of Perth for markets in the south. Upon his death in 1880 his son John also realised the future of the company was in London. When his brother Thomas joined the company four years later he was sent to London to open an office and begin making inroads.

In 1893 they were granted Queen Victoria's Royal Warrant for the supply of whisky to the royal household. As the demand for Dewar's whisky grew the brothers decided to do more than just blend and sell whisky. They took over the lease of Tullymet Distillery and built another distillery at Aberfeldy near the birthplace of their father.

While elder brother John managed production and administration, Thomas set off on a world tour to capture new markets. Over the course of two years he arranged shipments of whisky into countless ports worldwide. It was the basis for Dewar's export network which still exists today.

When the brothers died within a year of each other, Peter Dewar, no relation but a lifetime employee, was appointed chairman of the company in 1930. He consolidated North American markets for John Dewar and Sons Ltd and upon his death control was once again returned to the Dewar family.

Some fifteen years before Peter Dewar was appointed chairman the company had joined forces with one time rivals James Buchanan and Co Ltd. The arrangement saw the companies pool their profits and share the resources of each company. The companies retained their separate identities but together boasted the largest stock of maturing whisky in Scotland.

In 1925 the partnership merged with DCL. Some seven years earlier the trio had combined to acquire the Yoker grain distillery which fell silent two years after the 1925 amalgamation.

Over the ensuing years the new partnership dabbled in distillery ownership including the 1982 acquisition of the Ord Distillery in Ross-shire.

Using a process pioneered by John Dewar and Sons Ltd the distilling process involves mixing heather with the peat. The result is highly regarded malt marketed as Glenordie.

"Dewar's" matchstriker, Royal Doulton, 12cm (4¾") dia, AUS $300-350; US $200-230; £120-160.

These pages display a variety of glass decanters which were produced to promote Dewar's Scotch Whisky. All date back to the late nineteenth/early twentieth century. Most of the major distilleries commissioned glass manufacturers to produce similar decanters. However, these are now difficult to acquire in good condition and are under-rated on today's market values.

Above left: "Dewar's Imperial Scotch Whisky" red enamelled title, 28cm (11") high, AUS $300-400; US $200-250; £120-140.

Above centre: "Dewar's Scotch Whisky" etched gold title, 26cm (10¼") high, AUS $200-250; US $130-160; £80-100.

Above right: "Dewar's Whisky" etched gold title, 30cm (12") high, AUS $250-300; US $160-190; £100-120.

Far left: "Dewar's Scotch Whisky – By Royal Warrant to H.M. The King" etched gold title, 30cm (12") high, AUS $300-350; US $200-230; £120-140.

Left: "Dewar's Perth Whisky – By Royal Warrant to H.M. The Queen" etched gold title, 36cm (14") high, AUS $600-750; US $375-425; £250-300.

Above: "Dewar's Perth Whisky - By Royal Warrant to Her Majesty the Queen" large Royal Coat of Arms t'mark deep etched in gold, 28cm (11") high, AUS $300-350; US $200-230; £120-140.

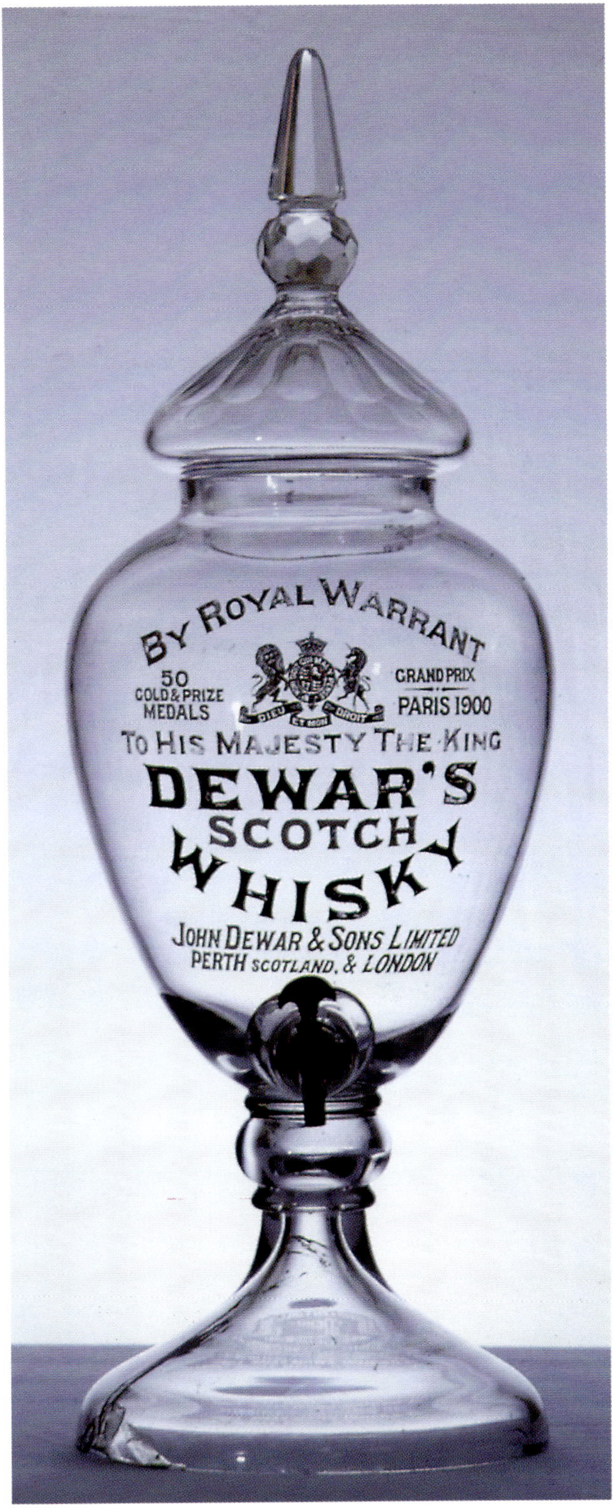

Right: Magnificent glass back bar dispenser, gold etched title advertsing "Dewar's Scotch Whisky – By Royal Warrant to his Majesty The King." Promotes the success of Dewar's Whisky world wide having won "50 gold & prize medals" including the "Grand Prix" (First Prize) at Paris in 1900. Height 70cm (28"), brass tap, AUS $3000-3500; US $2000-2300; £1200-1400.

Left: "John Dewar & Sons - Dewar's Perth Whisky" match-striker, Doulton Lambeth, 11.5cm (4½") dia, AUS $800-1000; US $500-650; £300-350.

Right: "Dewar's Whisky" matchstriker, Royal Doulton, 10cm (4") dia, AUS $700-900; US $400-450; £240-270.

Above left: Pastel blue "Dewar's Fine Scotch Whisky" Highland China, Scotland, 9cm (3½"), AUS $125-150; US $80-100; £50-60. **Centre:** Pastel blue "Dewar's Fine Scotch Whisky" Highland China, Scotland, 11cm (4½"), AUS $275-325; US $150-200; £75-100. **Right:** Pastel green "Dewar's Fine Scotch Whisky" Highland China, Scotland, 9cm (3½"), AUS $125-150; US $80-100; £50-60.

Below left: "Dewar's White Label Scotch Whisky" Diana, Australia, 14cm (5½"), AUS $120-150; US $100-130; £70-85. **Right:** "Dewar's White Label Scotch Whisky" Wade Regicor, 14cm (5½"), AUS $110-140; US $70-85; £45-55.

"Dewar's White Label Scotch Whisky" Wade Regicor, 10cm (4"), AUS $125-150; US $80-100; £50-65.

"Dewar's White Label Whisky" John Maddock & Sons, 11cm (4½"), AUS $175-225; US $110-130; £70-85.

"Dewar's Special Scotch Whisky" Wade Regicor, 13cm (5¼"), AUS $125-150; US $80-100; £50-65.

Above "Dewar's White Label" Royal Doulton, 11cm (4½"), AUS $300-350; US $200-250; £120-150.

Above centre & right: Two examples of the Elischer jug advertising "Dewar's Fine Scotch Whisky" 13.5cm (5¼") high. Initially this jug was produced in deep blue. However, a limited quantity is known to exist in other colours: white, green, black, yellow and pink. The more common blue version is valued at AUS $85-105; US $65-85; £40-50. The remaining seven colours would sell for AUS $130-160; US $85-100; £55-70.

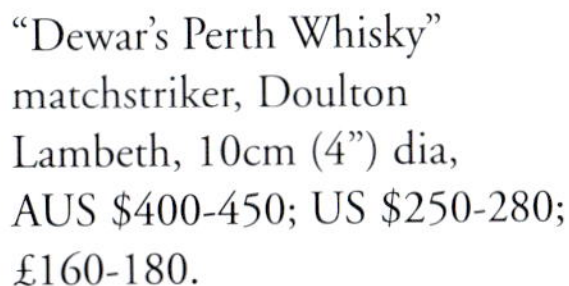

"Dewar's Perth Whisky" matchstriker, Doulton Lambeth, 10cm (4") dia, AUS $400-450; US $250-280; £160-180.

"Dewar's" matchstriker, Royal Doulton, 14cm (5½") dia, AUS $400-450; US $250-300; £150-180.

"Dewar's All Around The World" matchstriker, no base mark, 11cm (4½") high, AUS $550-700; US $350-425; £220-260.

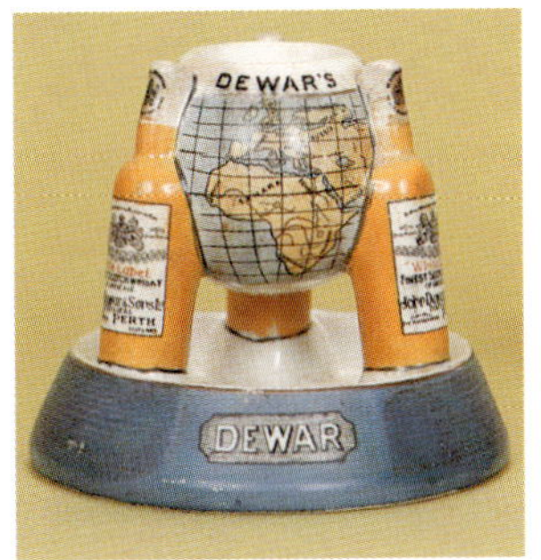

Colourful tin sign advertising "Dewar's Whisky" from the original painting by "Simpson" 37.5 x 28cm (14½" x 11"), AUS $400-500; US $250-300; £160-200.

"Dewar's Whisky" Royal Doulton, 17cm (6¾"), AUD $500-600; USD $325-385; £200-240.

Colourful tin sign advertising "Dewar's White Label" 38 x 28cm (15" x 11"), AUS $550-650; US $350-425; £220-260

Below left: Free standing tin sign advertising "Dewar's White Label Scotch Whisky" 53cm (21") high, AUS $300-350; US $200-230; £120-150. **Below right:** Tin serving tray advertising "Dewar's, The Whisky Of His Forefathers" 36cm (14") dia, AUS $400-500; US $250-300; £160-190.

"Dewar's Whisky" Doulton Lambeth stoneware jug, 18cm (7"), AUS $600-800; US $400-450; £250-300.

Above: Tin serving tray "Dewar's" whisky, 40 x 30cm (16 x 12") high, AUS $450-550; US $300-350; £175-225.

Left: "Dewar's White Label Whisky" menu holder, 6cm (2½"), AUS $150-200; US $100-125; £60-80.

Below left: "Dewar's Scotch Whisky" ashtray, Wade Regicor, 20cm x 12.5cm (8" x 5"), AUS $90-120; US $60-75; £35-40.

Below right: "Dewar's White Label" ashtray, Mintons, England, 12.5cm (5") dia, AUS $50-60; US $30-35; £20-25.

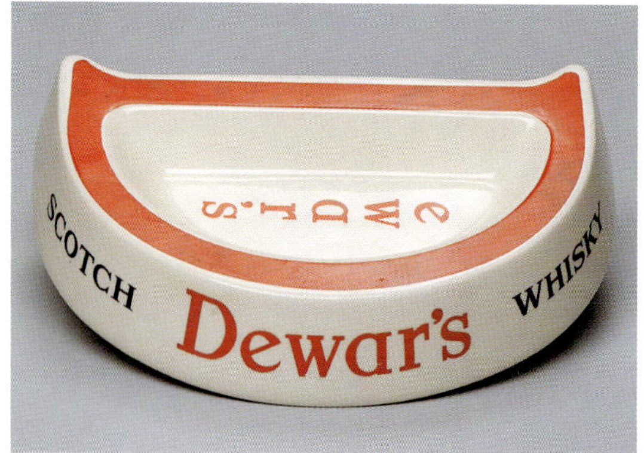

Right: "Dewar's" brass change tray, 15cm (6") dia, AUS $200-250; US $130-160; £80-100.

Left: "Dewar's White Label Scotch Whisky - It never varies" rubber compound figure on wooden base, 57cm (22½"), AUS $800-1000; US $500-650; £300-350.

Below: Three rubber compound Dewar's figures. **Left:** "Dewar's Scotch Whisky Never Varies" 24cm (9½"), AUS $150-200; US $100-130; £60-75. **Centre:** "Dewar's White Label Scotch Whisky - It Never Varies" 32.5cm (12¾"), AUS $450-550; US $300-350; £175-225. **Right:** "Dewar's Scotch Whisky" 24cm (9½"), AUS $100-125; US $65-80; £45-55.

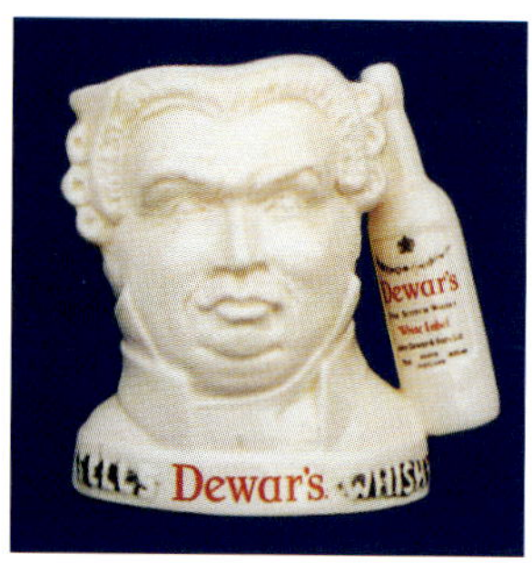

Left: "Dewar's White Label Scotch Whisky" Royal Doulton, 10cm (4"), AUS $450-650; US $300-350; £180-220.

Above: "Dewar's White Label Whisky" ashtray, John Maddock & Sons, 13cm (5¼") dia, AUS $65-85; US $40-50; £25-30.

Left: "Dewar's Scotch Whisky" ashtray, Diana, Australia, 15cm (6") wide, AUS $50-60; US $30-35; £20-25.

Left: "Dewar's White Label Scotch Whisky" ashbowl, Diana, Australia, 12cm (4¾") dia, AUS $50-60; US $30-35; £20-25.

Below: "Dewar's White Label" optic measure & bottle, height incl. bottle 50cm (17¾"), AUS $300-350; US $200-250; £120-150.

Below: Two Royal Doulton stoneware jugs "Dewar's Whisky" the small version 10.5cm (4½"), AUS $450-500; US $300-350; £180-210. The larger one at right 14cm (5½"), AUS $400-450; US $250-300; £160-190.

"Encore Scotch Whisky" S. Fielding & Co., (this example in poor cond.), 18cm (7"), value in good cond. AUS $700-850; US $400-500; £275-350.

"Edinburgh Castle Finest Scotch Whisky" Buchan Portobello, 16.5cm (6½"), AUS $80-100; US $50-60; £30-35.

"The Edradour Single Highland Malt Scotch Whisky" mini jug, no base mark, 8cm (3"), AUS $75-90; US $45-55; £20-25.

"Famous Grouse Scotch Whisky" Wade Regicor, 12.5cm (4¾"), rare version AUS $200-225; US $130-160; £80-100.

"The Famous Grouse Finest Scotch Whisky" Wade, 14.5cm (5¾"), AUS $80-100; US $50-60; £30-35.

"The Famous Grouse Finest Scotch Whisky" Piola, 15cm (6"), AUS $80-90; US $45-60; £30-35.

Below: Two jugs advertising "Frigate Rum" produced by Elischer, Australia, **left:** 15cm (6"), **right:** 16.5cm (6½"), each valued AUS $40-50; US $30-40; £25-30.

Below: "Fellsglen Scotch Whisky" Royal Doulton, 10.5cm (4¼"), AUS $450-550; US $300-350; £175-200.

"Fox & Co. Wine & Spirit Merchant" Made in England, 13cm (5¼"), AUS $700-850; US $450-550; £250-300.

"William Foulds" enamel ashtray, 13.5cm (5¼"), AUS $80-100; US $50-60; £30-40.

"Four Crown Sovereign Whisky" ashtray, James Green & Nephew, 13cm (5¼"), AUS $180-220; US $110-130; £70-85.

Above left: "Golden Eagle Liqueur Scotch Whisky - Friary Brewery" Minton Regicor, 11.5cm (4½"), AUS $350-400; US $225-250; £140-170. **Above right:** "Four Roses Bourbon" San Claudio, 20cm (8"), AUS $65-75; US $40-50; £25-30.

Below left: "Glen Garry Finest Scotch Whisky" Ventura, 10.5cm (4¼"), AUS $225-250; US $140-170; £90-110. **Below centre:** "Glenfalloch Highland Whisky" W & AK Johnston Glasgow, 12cm (4¾"), AUS $600-700; US $375-400; £240-270. **Below right:** "Glen Garry Scotch Whisky" West Highland Pottery, 10cm (4"), AUS $175-200; US $110-130; £70-85.

1950's paper magazine advertisement for "Gilbeys Spey-Royal Whisky."

Glenlivet

It may be just on thirty years since the company Glenlivet Distillers Ltd was formed but its roots extend back into the 1800s.

Glenlivet Distillers Ltd is the group name adopted by Glenlivet and Glen Grant distilleries in 1970. The company consists of production, marketing and sales divisions.

Glenlivet Distillers Ltd owns five Highland malt distilleries widely considered to produce some of the best malt whiskies on the market.

The 1970 merger signalled a period of heavy investment and subsequent growth for Glenlivet Distillers Ltd. The company invested in its distilleries, bottling/blending plant and by-product plants with a subsequent increase in distilling capacity of 58 percent.

Some of Glenlivet Distillers Ltd subsidiaries include Longmorn Distillers Ltd, George and JG Smith, J and J Grant, Glen Grant Ltd, the Glenlivet Whisky Company Ltd, Seafield Blending Company, JM Tulloch and Company Ltd along with Turner and Nicol Ltd. Since 1978, it has been a wholly owned subsidiary of Seagram Co Ltd of Canada.

"The Glenlivet -12 Years Old" Set of three jugs, Highland China, Scotland, 15cm, 11cm and 9 cm (6″ 4½″ and 3½″), AUS $75-90; US $45-55; £30-35 each.

Below left: "Arrowsmith's Glenlivet Blend" S. Fielding & Co, 10cm (4″), AUS $650-850; US $400-450; £250-300. **Below right:** "Craigellachie Glenlivet Distillery" no base mark, 14.5cm (5½″), AUS $1250-1500; US $800-1000; £500-600.

Above left: "Glenlivet" Piola, 16.5cm (6½″), AUS $125-150; US $80-100; £50-60.
Above centre: "Glenlivet" San Claudio, 12cm (4¾″), AUS $75-90; US $50-60; £30-35.
Above right: "Glenlivet" Wade, 14.5cm (5¾″), AUS $170-200; US $100-125; £65-75.

Left: "Glen Deveron" Piola, 9cm (3½″), AUS $90-110; US $60-70; £35-40.

Below: Tin serving tray "Gilmour Thomson's Scotch Whiskies" 40 x 30cm (16 x 12″), AUS $500-600; US $325-375, £200-250.

Below: "Glenlivet" no base mark, 17cm (6¾″), AUS $100-120; US $65-75; £40-50.

Below: Miniature "Glenalmond Highland Malt Scotch Whisky" Buchan Portobello, 8cm (3¼″), AUS $90-110; US $50-60; £30-35.

"Glenfiddich Single Malt Scotch Whisky" Highland China, Scotland, 13cm (5¼"), AUS $120-150; US $80-100; £50-60.

"Glenfiddich Single Malt Scotch Whisky" no base stamp, 7cm (2¾"), AUS $55-65; US $35-40; £20-25.

"Glenmorangie Single Highland Malt Whisky" Buchan Portobello, 11.5cm (4½"), AUS $120-150; US $80-90; £50-60.

Below: "Glenfiddich" plaster figure, 34cm (13¼"), AUS $800-1000; US $500-600; £325-375.

Above: "Gilbey's" Wade Regicor, 17.5cm (6¾"), AUS $130-150; US $80-90; £50-60.

Below: "Glenfarclas" Euroceramics, 14cm (5½"), AUS $75-90; US $50-60; £30-35.

"Grant's" no base mark, 15cm (6″), AUS $80-100; US $50-60; £30-35.

"Grant's" no base mark, triangular bodied, 10cm (4″), AUS $225-250; US $140-160; £90-110.

"Grant's" HCW, 15.5cm (6″), AUS $90-110; US $60-70; £35-40.

"Grant's" Carter Adv. Supply Co., 12cm (4¾″), AUS $275-325; US $180-200; £110-130.

"Grant's Scotch Whisky" triangular bodied, Wade Regicor, 10cm (4″), AUS $175-200; US $110-130; £70-80.

Chocolate brown "Grant's Royal Scotch Whisky" Wade, 15cm (6″), AUS $175-200; US $110-130; £70-85.

"Grant's" Wade Regicor, 10cm (4″), AUS $110-130; US $70-80; £45-55.

"Grant's" Invercauld, no base mark, 14.5cm (5¾″), AUS $450-550; US $300-350; £175-200.

"Glen Grant Distillery - 150th Anniversary" Balfour China, Scotland, 13.5cm (5¼″), AUS $200-225; US $130-160; £80-100.

Above left: "Grant's Invercauld Scotch" no base mark, 14cm (5½"), AUS $1700-2000; US $1000-1250; £700-850. **Above right:** "Greyhound Special Scotch Whisky" produced for Mackie's, Fielding, 11cm (4½"), AUS $2000-2500; US $1300-1600; £800-1000.

Below: Two porcelain figures advertising "Greenlees": Left: "Greenlees Claymore The Favourite Scotch Everywhere" 40cm (15¾"),Right: "Greenlees Brothers Ancient Old Parr Antique Scotch Whisky" 40cm (15¾"). Both valued at AUS $4000-4500; US $2600-3000; £1600-1800.

Below: "Greenlees Rare Old Scotch Whiskies" no base mark, 11cm (4½"), AUS $400-450; US $250-300; £160-180.

Above: "Guinness Dog's Head/Bass" match-striker, Read Bros, London, 14 x 13cm (5½ x 5″), AUS $800-1000; US $500-600; £320-350.

Above: Ceramic clock, "Opening Time Is Guinness Time" 41 x 33cm (16″ x 13″), AUS $150-175; US $100-120; £50-60.

Left: "Guinness For Strength" no base mark, 11cm (4½″), AUS $40-50; US $25-30; £15-20.

Below: Plastic Leprechaun advertising "Guinness Foreign Extra Stout" 39 x 30cm (15½ x 12″), AUS $1000-1250; US $600-700; £400-450.

Below: "Guinness" plastic figure, features an unopened bottle of "Guinness Foreign Extra Stout" 23cm (9″), AUS $200-250; US $125-150; £80-100.

"Harvey's" Gray's Pottery, 11.5cm (4½"), AUS $175-200; US $110-130; £70-80.

"Harvey's Special" Carlton Ware, 8cm (3"), AUS $500-600; US $325-350; £200-225.

"H & S Special Scotch Whisky" James Green & Nephew, 10.5cm (4¼"), AUS $400-450; US $250-300; £160-180.

"House Of Lords" Wade, 14cm (5½"), AUS $125-150; US $80-90; £50-60.

"Huntsman Ales" James Green & Nephew, 10cm (4"), AUS $600-700; US $375-450; £240-280.

"Highland Queen" Buchan Portobello, 13cm (5¼"), AUS $80-100; US $50-60; £30-35.

"Hewitt's Whisky" Arklow Pottery, 12cm (4¾"), AUS $150-175; US $100-120; £60-70.

"Highland Queen" Minton, 12cm (4¾"), AUS $400-450; US $260-290; £160-180.

"House Of Lords Scotch Whisky" Wade, 16cm (6¼"), AUS $110-130; US $70-80; £45-50.

"Highland Laddie Old Scotch Whisky" Causton & Sons, 12cm (4¾″), AUS $1000-1250; US $650-750; £400-500.

Rubber compound "Hennessy Cognac" bar figure, 26cm (10¼″)high, AUS $600-750; US $400-450; £250-300.

"Highland Fusilier Finest Scotch Whisky" Euroceramics, twice the size of normal jugs, 23cm (9″), AUS $200-250; US $130-160; £80-100.

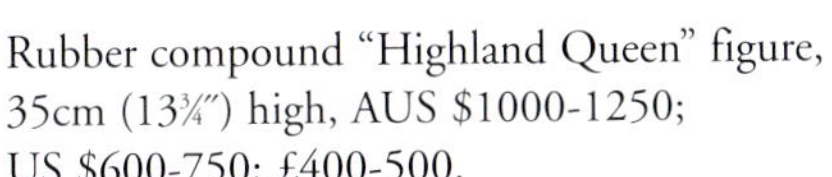

Rubber compound "Highland Queen" figure, 35cm (13¾″) high, AUS $1000-1250; US $600-750; £400-500.

"Harvey's Special Scotch Whisky" Shelley, 14cm (5½″), AUS $600-700; US $400-450; £250-275.

Haig's

Haig's has a long association with Scotch whisky spanning more than 300 years. The first reference linking the Haig family and distilling was the appearance of Robert Haig before the Kirk Session in 1655 when he was accused of operating his still on the Sabbath. Many farmers operated their own stills and the beginning of the Haig tradition is believed to have started with the purchase of farming land at Throsk in 1627.

Their distilling enterprise blossomed when Robert Haig's great grandson John married into the Stein family – owners of a number of distilleries and pioneers of the whisky trail to London.

While each of John's sons helped continue the family's whisky making tradition it was the work of his youngest son William which led to the creation of the House of Haig. He took over a distillery at Seggie, control of which went to his youngest son Robert. William's eldest son John established his own distillery at Cameron Bridge and set about building up its reputation.

After World War 1 DCL acquired the entire ordinary share capital which led to considerable rebuilding and expansion. In 1923 DCL also acquired Haig and Haig Ltd, formerly controlled by Robertson and Baxter Ltd.

Two years later the new acquisition became a wholly owned subsidiary of John Haig. By 1939 Haig was the biggest selling whisky brand in Britain.

Above left: "Haig 5 Star" no base stamp, 10cm (4"), AUS $200-250; US $130-160; £80-100. **Right:** "Haig" Carlton Ware, 9cm (3½"), AUS $175-200; US $110-130; £70-80.

Below: Three variations of "Haig" jugs. The jug at left is relatively common. **Left:** "Haig" Carlton Ware, 9cm (3½"), AUS $75-90; US $50-60; £30-35. **Centre:** "Haig" Carlton Ware, 10cm (4"), AUS $175-200; US $110-130; £70-80. **Right:** "Haig" Carlton Ware, 9cm (3½"), AUS $175-200; US $110-130; £70-80.

"Haig" Made in England, recent jug produced in three sizes, this one is 16cm (6¼") high, AUS $90-110; US $55-65; £30-35.

Brass ashtray "Haig & Haig Scotch Whisky" 12cm (4¾") dia, AUS $75-100; US $50-60; £30-35.

"Haig" Made in England, recent jug produced in three sizes, this one is 20.5cm (8") high, AUS $90-110; US $55-65; £30-35.

Right: "Haig" Wade, 16.5cm (6½"), AUS $100-120; US $65-75; £40-50.

Left: "Haig Scotch Whisky" no base mark, 19cm (7½"), AUS $65-75; US $50-60; £30-35.

Below Right: "Haig & Haig Whisky" Royal Doulton, 14cm (5½"), AUS $750-900; US $500-600; £300-350.

Below: "Haig & Haig Three Star Scotch Whisky" matchstriker, W.H. Waller & Co., London, 11cm (4¼") dia, AUS $150-175; US $100-120; £60-75.

"Inver House Green Plaid Rare Scotch Whisky" Wade, 17.5cm (7″), AUS $80-100; US $50-60; £30-35.

"Jameson Irish Whiskey" Piola, 12cm (4¾″), AUS $75-90; US $50-60; £30-35.

"Inver House" Euroceramics, 20cm (8″), AUS $80-100; US $50-60; £30-35.

"Jameson Red Seal Whiskey" Arklow, 9.5cm (3¾″), AUS $175-200; US $110-130; £70-80.

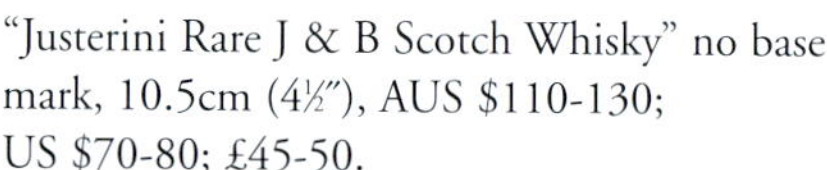

"Justerini Rare J & B Scotch Whisky" no base mark, 10.5cm (4½″), AUS $110-130; US $70-80; £45-50.

"Ind. Coope & Co Ltd. Brewers" matchstriker, 8 x 14.5cm (3¼ x 5¾″), AUS $400-450; US $250-300; £160-190.

"Jameson Irish Whiskey" no base mark, 5.5cm (2"), AUS $90-110; US $60-70; £35-40.

"Jameson Irish Whiskey" no base mark, 10cm (4"), AUS $175-200; US $110-130; £70-85.

"John Jameson Whiskey" James Green & Nephew, 15.5cm (6"), AUS $425-475; US $275-300; £170-200.

"King George IV - Monarch Of All Whiskies" ashbowl, Made in England, 11.5 x 8.5cm (4½" x 3¼"), AUS $175-225; US $110-130; £70-85.

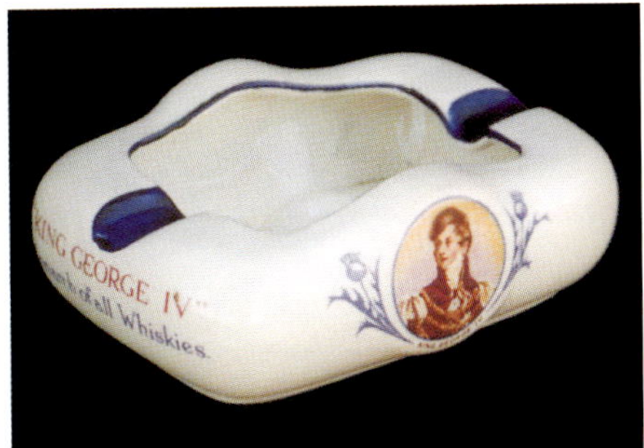

Below: Three "King George IV Scotch Whisky" jugs,
Left: HCW, 14cm (5½"), AUS $325-365; US $210-230; £130-150. **Centre:** Moulin Des Loups, France, 14cm (5½"), AUS $600-700; US $325-350; £200-225. **Right:** Wade, 11cm (4½"), AUS $250-300; US $160-185; £100-120.

Above left: "King George IV" Gray's Pottery, 19.5cm (7½″), AUS $500-600; US $325-350; £200-225. **Above right:** Ruby glass jug advertising "King George IV Scotch Whisky" 20cm (8″), AUS $1000-1200; US $600-700; £400-450.

Left: "King George IV" rubber compound figure, 36cm (14″), AUS $325-400; US $210-250; £125-150.

Below: "King George IV" Royal Doulton, 15cm (6″), AUS $800-1000; US $500-600; £320-360.

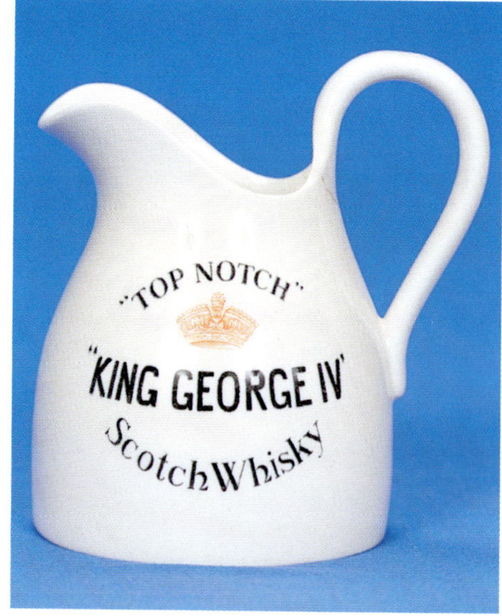

"King George IV" Distillers Agency, 10cm (4″), AUS $450-500; US $300-350; £175-200.

"Kinloch's" Fieldings, Stoke-On-Trent, 15cm (6″), AUS $1000-1250; US $650-750; £400-450.

Above: "King George IV Top Notch" match-holder/ashtray, Royal Doulton, 12cm (4¾″) dia, AUS $350-400; US $225-250; £130-160.

Above: "King Of Kings, Rare Old De Luxe Scotch Whisky" Wade Regicor, 11.5cm (4½″), AUS $200-230; US $130-160; £80-100.

"Lairds" no base mark, halfsize, 11cm (4½″), AUS $70-85; USA $45-60; £30-35.

"Lang's Supreme Scotch Whisky" Wade PDM, 15cm (6″), AUS $175-225; US $110-130; £70-85.

"Lang's Supreme" Made in France, 13cm (5½″), AUS $125-150; US $80-100; £50-60.

"Loch Corrie" Wade Regicor, 16cm (6¼″), AUS $150-175; US $100-125; £60-70.

"Longman Scotch Whiskey" Wade, 15cm (6″), AUS $150-180; US $100-200; £60-70.

"Laphroaig" Piola, 16cm (6¼″), AUS $65-75; US $40-50; £25-30.

"Long John" ashbowl, Impressed Mark "England" 6 x 8cm (2½ x 3¼″), AUS $150-175; US $95-110; £50-60.

"Long John" James Green & Nephew, 17cm (6¾″), AUS $400-450; US $250-275; £150-175.

"Long John" Seton Pottery, 17cm (6¾″), AUS $200-250; US $130-160; £80-100.

Below: "Lowrie Scotch Whisky" Wilkinson Ltd. England, 9cm (3½″), AUS $550-650; US $350-375; £220-250.

Below: "Lowrie Scotch Whisky" Made in England, 12cm (4¾″), AUS $400-450; US $250-275; £150-175.

Elischer's McCallum Jugs:

Prior to 1991 the only variations known of "The McCallum" character jugs were the coloured Wade variations, the mustard yellow Elischer sets and the coloured and white Royal Doulton large size examples. Most of the different colour variations produced by Elischer have only recently been discovered and are now eagerly sought by collectors. We know of approximately twenty different colour variations with price depending on the quality of detail on the faces. Colours known are: White, natural (cream), light grey, dark grey, burgandy, plum, olive green, dark green, vibrant green, corn (light) blue, dark blue, mustard yellow (the original colour), light brown, dark brown, custard yellow, lavendar, black, charcoal (matt). As far as we can ascertain only a few sets were produced of each colour, the most common colour being the mustard yellow version which was made over a number of years by Elischer.

Above: Rare set of the grey "McCallum" character jugs. Value AUS $200-250; US $130-160; £80-100 each. Many of the other colourways also command this value, price being determined by facial definition. A lower value of AUS $90-120; US $60-80; £40-50 applies to those colourways featuring thick glaze which virtually obliterates definition. **Below:** Other colour variations, values fluctuate between AUS $100-250; US $65-160; £40-100 each. Note that size does not have any influence on value.

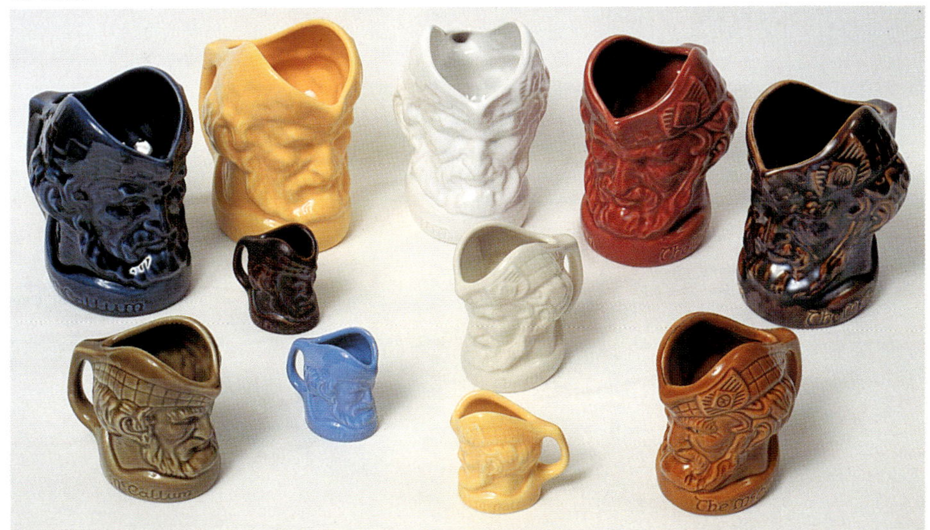

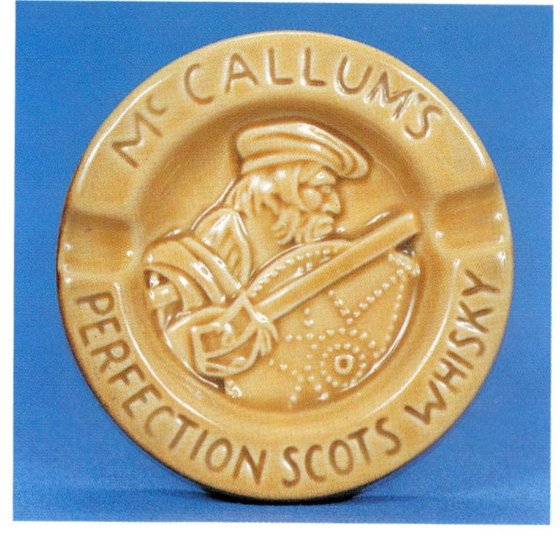

Above left: "McCallum's Perfection Scots Whisky" Made in Spain, 19cm (7″), AUS $70-85; US $45-55; £25-30.

Above right: "McCallum's Perfection Scots Whisky" ashtray, no base mark, 11cm (4½″) dia, AUS $50-70; US $30-35; £20-25.

Left: "McCallum's Perfection Scots Whisky" labelled bottle with "nip" cap, 10cm (4″), AUS $50-70; US $30-40; £20-25.

Below: Matching Royal Doulton jug and ashbowl advertising "McCallum's Perfection Scots Whisky" Jug 12cm (4¾″) high, AUS $220-250; US $140-165; £90-110.
Ashbowl 11.5 x 4cm (4½ x 1¾″), AUS $125-150; US $80-100; £50-60.

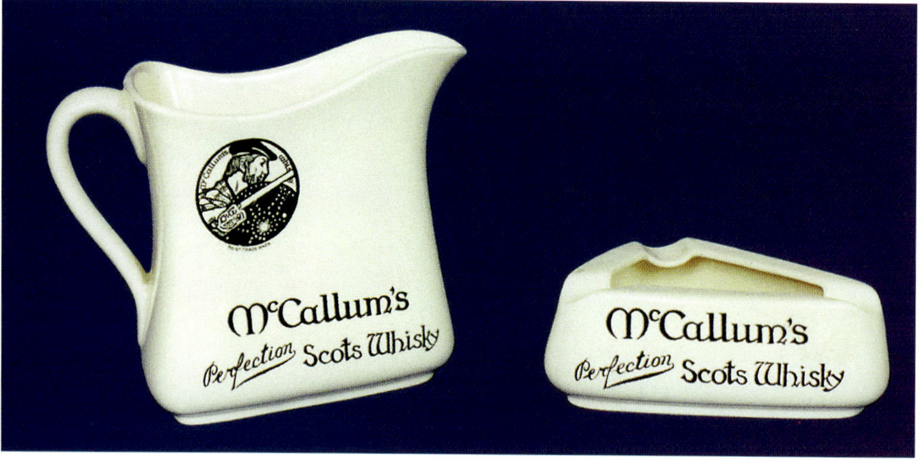

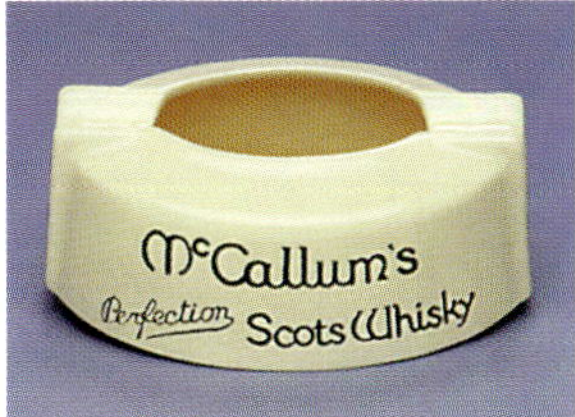

Top: "McCallum's Perfection Scots Whisky" ashbowl, Elischer, 15 x 4.5cm (6 x 1¾"), AUS $20-25; US $15-20; £10-15.
Above: "McCallum's Perfection Scots Whisky" ashbowl, Wade Regicor, oval base 12 x 9 x 4.5cm (4¾ x 3½ x 1¾"), AUS $60-80; US $40-50; £25-30.

Right: Glass back bar bottle "McCallum's Perfection Whisky" glass stopper, brass tap, 50cm (20") high, AUS $1500-2000; US $1000-1250; £600-800.

Below left: "D. & J. McCallum's Perfection Scotch Whisky" no base mark, 12.5 cm, (5") high, AUS $800-1000; US $500-600; £300-350.

Below right: "McCallum's Whisky" tin serving tray, 25cm (10"), AUS $50-70; US $30-40; £20-25.

Above: "MacNish Very Light Scotch" no base mark, 16.5cm (6½"), AUS $175-200; US $110-130; £70-85.

Below: "The Great Macaulay Blended Scotch Whisky" Euroceramics, 18cm (7"), twice the capacity of normal jugs, AUS $150-175; US $100-120; £60-75.

Above: "McNish's Special Scotch Whisky" rubber compound figure, 41cm (16") high, AUS $1250-1500; US $800-1000; £500-600.

Below: Two versions of "The Macallan Single Highland Malt Scotch Whisky" both produced in Barcelona, 17cm (6¾"), AUS $75-85; US $50-60; £30-35.

Below: Full deck of "McCallum's" playing cards, AUS $125-150; US $80-95; £50-60.

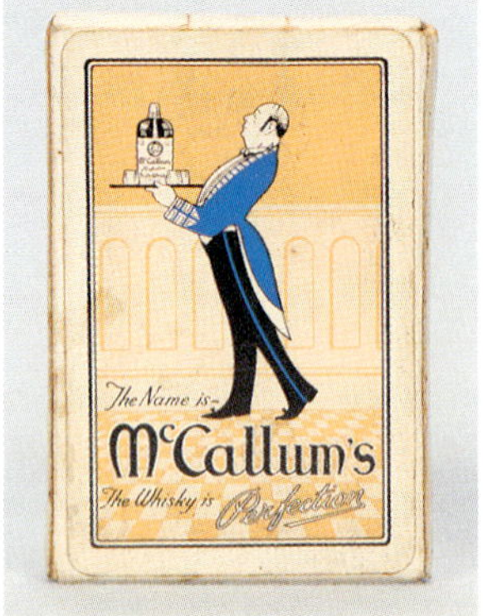

Below: "Meynell Hunt Scotch Whisky" Anchor, England, 11.5cm (4½"), AUS $700-900; US $450-600; £275-300.

Above left: Miniature "The Macallan Single Highland Malt Scotch Whisky" no base stamp, 7cm (2¾") high, AUS $80-95; US $50-60; £25-30. HCW also produced an identical white version but with a slight variation in colours. Value for this type is AUS $90-110; US $60-70; £35-40.

Above right: Standard size "The Macallan - The Secret" HCW, 15cm (6"), AUS $90-110; US $60-70; £35-40.

Below left: "Morrison's Glengarioch Distillery" Buchan Portobello, 15.5cm (6"), AUS $90-110; US $60-70; £35-40.

Below right: "Mansfield Ales" Made in England, 9cm (3½"), AUS $500-600; US $300-350; £200-230.

Above: "McNish's Special Scotch Whisky" James Green & Nephew, 10cm (4″), AUS $500-550; US $325-375; £200-250.

Above: "Dan MacFarlane's Royal V.O.V. Scotch Whisky" ashtray, 13cm (5″), AUS $40-50; US $25-30; £25-30.

Upper centre: "McKibbins" Arklow, 10.5cm (4¼″), AUS $100-125; US $60- 75; £40-50.

Lower centre: "Macnish Scotch Whiskies" HCW, 10.25cm (4¼″), AUS $220-250; US $140-165; £90-110.

Below: "McMullens Scottish Chief Whisky" J. Clifton Cottle London, 11cm (4½″), AUS $400-500; US $250-280; £160-180.

Below: "McNish" ashtray, Dunn Bennett & Co Burslem, 15 x 10cm (6 x 4″), AUS $200-250; US $130-160; £80-100.

Above: Both sides of a jug advertising "Macbeth Scotch Whisky" limited edition of 500 produced during the 1960s, base impressed. Lord Nelson, England. Height 17.5cm (7"), AUS $200-250; US $130-160; £80-100.

Right: "Morton's Old Scotch Whiskies" Wade Regicor, 10cm (4"), AUS $200-230; US $130-160; £80-90.

Below left: "Mackinlay's Liqueur Scotch Whisky" 10cm (4"), AUS $600-700; US $375-450; £240-260.

Below right: "Macpherson's Cluny Very Old Liqueur Scotch Whisky" no base mark, 9cm (3½"), AUS $250-300; US $160-185; £100-125.

Macleay Duff

Macleay Duff (Distillers) Ltd owns, under licence, Millburn Distillery on the outskirts of Inverness. Millburn is one of the earliest legal distilleries, established in 1807. It survived competition from illegal whisky makers and smugglers to prosper from the mid 1820s onwards.

In 1853 corn merchant David Rose purchased the property and just over twenty years later he extensively rebuilt and enlarged the distillery. His son George took over the running of Millburn in 1881 and one year later it changed hands again, this timc to two members of the Haig family.

Millburn Distillery became Haig and Company, Distillers, Millburn but in 1904 reverted simply to Millburn Distillery Company.

When the distillery changed hands again in 1921 the success was to be shortlived. Fire damaged most of the major buildings necessitating a complete redesign of the entire distillery.

In 1933 Millburn joined the DCL family and ten years later was transferred to Scotch Malt Distillers Ltd.

Right: "Macleay Duff Scotch Whisky" rubber compound figure, produced in 1963 to commemorate the centenary of the distillery, 22cm (8¾"), AUS $400-450; US $250-280; £150-175.

Above: "Macleay Duff Scotch Whisky" Wade Regicor, 10cm (4"), AUS $90-110; US $60-70; £35-40.

Above: "Andy MacDuff Blended Scotch Whisky" Ceramiques, 13.5cm (5¼"), AUS $80-100; US $50-60; £30-35.

Above: "MacPherson's Cluny Scotch Whisky" rubber compound figure, 21cm (8¼"), AUS $800-1000; US $500-600; £325-375.

Below: "Andy MacDuff Blended Scotch Whisky" Euroceramics, 14cm (5½"), AUS $80-100; US $50-60; £30-35.

Below: "Andy MacDuff Blended Scotch Whisky" Euroceramics, 13cm (5"), AUS $90-110; US $60-70; £35-40.

Above: "Mackinlay's Scotch Whisky" James Green & Nephew, 10cm (4″), AUS $300-350; US $200-250; £120-140.

Above right: "Mackinlay's Finest Old Scotch Whisky" HCW, 13cm (5¼″), AUS $100-120; US $65-75; £40-50.

Right: "Mackinlay's Scotch Whisky" Wade Regicor, 13cm, (5¼″), AUS $150-175; US $100-125; £60-100.

Below left: "Mackinlay's Scotch Whisky" rubber compound figure, 36cm (14″), AUS $1000-1250; US $650-750; £400-500.

Below right: "Mackinlay" rubber compound bar figure, 16.5cm (6½″) high, AUS $450-550; US $300-350; £180-220.

Tin calendar "MacKinlay's Scotch Whisky" 31 x 24cm (12 x 9½"), AUS $400-450; US $250-280; £150-175.

Above: Three different "Mitchells & Butlers" jugs." Clan Ivor" "Bally Boy" and "Dumbarton" all T.G. Green & Co., each 11cm (4¼") high. The "Clan Ivor" and "Dumbarton" AUS $500-600; US $300-350; £200-230. The "Bally Boy" valued AUS $700-900; US $450-500; £275-300.

Right: "Milne's Pharlap Whisky" plaster figure, 30cm (11¾"), AUS $1500-2000; US $1000-1250; £600-800.

Below left: "Munro's King Of Kings Rare Old De Luxe Scotch Whisky" Highland China, Scotland, 9cm (3½"), AUS $170-200; US $100-125; £60-75.

Below right: "Munro's Dalwhinnie Whisky" counter bell, AUS $350-400; US $225-250; £140-165.

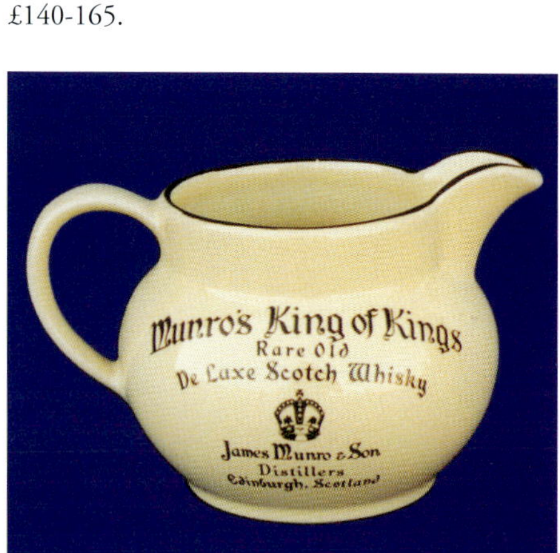

Left: "Ye Monks Scots Whisky" Wade Regicor, 11cm (4¼"), AUS $220-250; US $140-165; £90-110.

Right: "Murdoch's Blended Scotch Whisky" Buchan Portobello, 12cm (4¾"), AUS $75-90; US $50-60; £30-35.

"Old Guns Finest Scotch Whisky" Wade Regicor, 19cm (7½"), AUS $300-350; US $200-230; £125-150.

"Offilers' Ales" no base mark, 9cm (3½"), AUS $500-600; US $300-350; £200-250.

"Oldfield's Blue Label Scotch Whisky" Wade Regicor, 14cm (5½"), AUS $125-150; US $80-100; 50-60.

"Old Mull Fine Scotch Whisky" Wade, 10cm (4"), AUS $80-100; US $50-60; £40-45.

"Old Court Blended Scotch Whisky" Wade, 12cm (4¾"), AUS $90-120; US $55-65; £35-40.

Old Bushmills

Old Bushmills is renowned for its high quality and fine flavour. It is made from a unique blend of one malt and one grain whiskey, a combination which sets it apart from its competitors.

The distillery itself is the oldest in the world and still draws its water from the same source today as the very first batch of this unique whiskey.

A representative of King James I officially instituted the Bushmills distillery but references to distillation on the site go back as far as 1494.

Ownership of the distillery has changed frequently over the years. From the mid 1880s right through until the late 1940s the distillery was owned by the Boyd family and was known as the Old Bushmills Distillery Company Ltd.

In 1964 Bass Charrington purchased the distillery, subsequently selling it to Seagram. Irish Distillers obtained a controlling interest and in 1978 acquired Seagram's remaining 20 percent interest. Just over twenty years ago the distillery was expanded and output increased.

Above left: "Old Bushmills Famous For Over 300 Years" J.A. Campbell, Belfast, 9cm (3½"), AUS $350-400; US $225-255; £140-165. **Above centre:** "Old Bushmills Pure Malt Whiskey" match-holder, Fielding, 9cm (3½"), AUS $250-300; US $160-190; £100-120. **Above right:** "Old Bushmills Pure Malt Whiskey" J.A. Campbell, Belfast, 10cm (4"), AUS $400-450; US $250-275; £150-175.

Below left: "Old Grandad Bourbon" cameo portrait, US Distillers name on base, 16cm (6¼"), AUS $200-250; US $125-150; £80-100. **Below centre:** "Old Bushmills Whiskey" Wade Regicor, 11.5cm (4¾"), AUS $175-200; US $110-130; £70-85. **Right:** "Old Bushmills Pure Malt Whiskey" Hillchurch Pottery, 22.5cm (9"), AUS $175-200; US $100-125; £50-65.

Above left: "Old Mull Scotch Whisky" Gray's Pottery, 7.5cm (2¾"), AUS $300-350; US $200-225; £120-140. **Above centre:** "O.V.H. Old Scotch Whisky" Made in England, 10.5cm (4¼"), AUS $600-700; US $375-425; £225-250. **Above right:** "Bushmills Irish Whiskey" Irish Distillers, 16.5cm (6½"), AUS $90-110; US $60-70; £35-40.

Left: "Passport Scotch" San Claudio, 20cm (8"), AUS $75-90; US $50-60; £30-35.

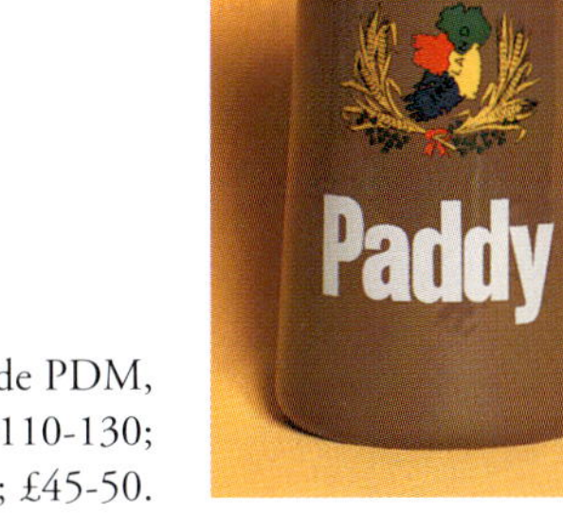

Right: "Paddy" Wade PDM, 16cm (6¼"), AUS $110-130; US $70-85; £45-50.

Below left: "Phoenix Special Scotch" Causton & Son, 10cm (4"), AUS $700-800; US $450-500; £275-300. **Below right:** "Pattisons' Scotch Whisky" Port Dundas stoneware, 17.5cm (7"), AUS $800-1000; US $500-600; £300-350.

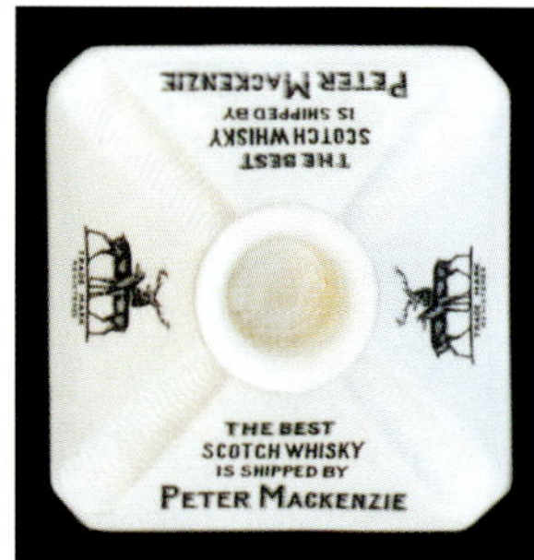

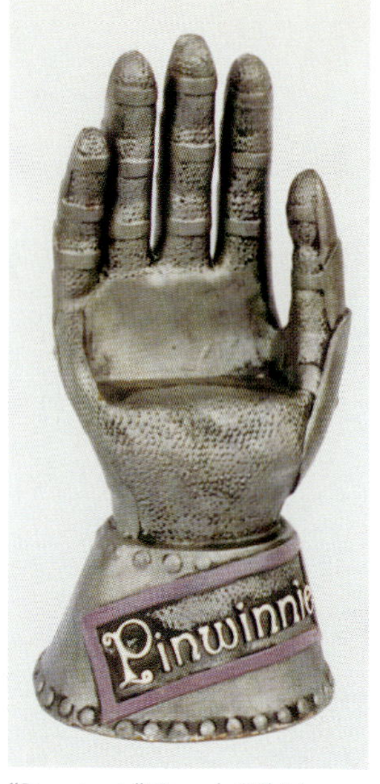

"Pinwinnie" Scotch Whisky, rubber compound figure, 28cm (11″), AUS $300-350; US $200-250; £120-150

Above left: "Peter Mackenzie The Best Scotch Whisky" match-striker, S. Fielding & Co., 13cm (5″) square, AUS $250-300; US $175-200; £100-125.

Above centre: "Peters Crown Seal Whisky" J. Clifton Cottle & Son, London, 10cm (4″), AUS $300-350; US $200-230; £120-145.

Above left: "Pickwick Fine Old Scotch Whisky" Royal Crawford Ironstone, 14cm (5½″), AUS $200-250; US $125-150; £80-100. **Above centre:** "Pinwinnnie Royale Scotch Whisky" Piola, 18cm (7″), AUS $60-75; US $40-50; £25-30.

Below left: "Paget Special Scotch Whisky" Price Bristol, 12cm (4¾″), AUS $300-350; US $200-225; £120-150. **Below centre:** "President Special Reserve De Luxe Scotch Whisky" Wade, 12cm (4¾″), AUS $220-250; US $125-150; £80-100. **Below right:** "Prince Charlie Scotch Whisky" Royal Norfolk, 14cm (5½″), AUS $225-250; US $150-175; £90-110.

Queen Anne

The name "Queen Anne" was chosen for Hill Thomson and Co's signature brand because it represented a time of great prosperity and endeavour in the history of Britain.

Hill Thomson and Co had its humble beginnings back in 1793 when William Hill opened a licensed grocer's shop in Edinburgh. The business prospered and upon William's death was taken over by two of his sons. When they died a third son assumed control in 1837.

Twenty years later the company went into partnership with William Thomson and assumed the name it operates under today. It was then that the business began seriously blending and bottling their own brands of whisky.

Twenty years later Robert Shaw joined the company. He began promoting the brand of whisky he called "Queen Anne." In 1939 his sons joined the company and began promoting the brand even further. A new generation followed in their footsteps until 1970 when Hill Thomson and Co merged with a number of other distilling interests to form The Glenlivet Distillers Ltd.

"Queen Anne" became the group's signature brand. The merger also allowed its makers to have first call on the companies' five malt whiskies including Glenlivet and Glen Grant.

Some of the subsidiaries which formed part of Hill Thomson and Co during its independent days still exist under the present structure.

Three "Queen Anne Scotch Whisky" bar figures, **Left:** Plastic figure 24cm (9½") high, AUS $450-550; US $250-300; £160-180. **Centre:** Rubber compound figure, 29cm (11½") high, AUS $900-1200; US $550-650; £350-400. **Right:** Rubber compound figure, 19cm (7½"), AUS $650-750; US $425-475; £250-300.

Left:
"Red Crown Rum" figure, Plastos Australia, 29cm (11¼″), AUS $700-850; US $450-550; £275-325.

Right:
Rubber compound figure "Red Hackle - Scotland's Best Whisky" 44cm (17½″), AUS $1000-1250; US $600-700; £400-500.

Far left: "Red Crown Special Scotch Whisky" 14.5cm (5½″), AUS $650-800; US $425-475; £275-325.

Left: "Red Hackle Scotch Whisky" Empire Works England, 10cm (4″), AUS $400-450; US $250-300; £150-175.

Bottom left: "Ridlington's Black Pear Scotch Whisky" Royal Doulton, 10cm (4″), AUS $450-525; US $300-350; £175-210. **Bottom centre:** "Royal Canadian" Imported By Barclay & Co, 15cm (6″), AUS $200-250; US $125-150; £80-100. **Bottom right:** "Roderick Dhu" matchstriker, W. Brownlie & Co Glasgow, 11cm (4½″) dia, AUS $800-1000; US $500-600; £325-400.

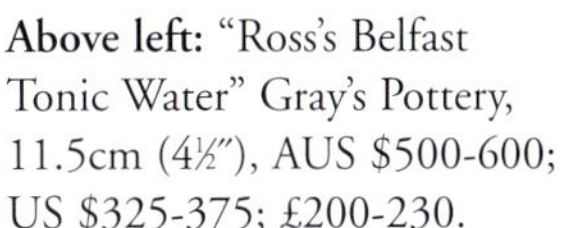

Above left: "Ross's Belfast Tonic Water" Gray's Pottery, 11.5cm (4½"), AUS $500-600; US $325-375; £200-230.

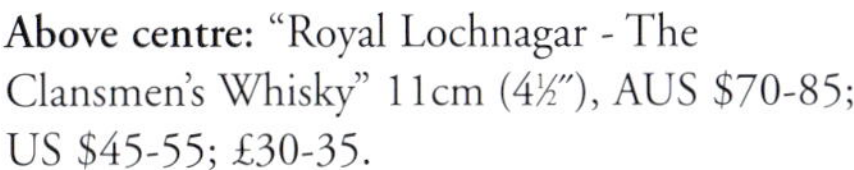

Above centre: "Royal Lochnagar - The Clansmen's Whisky" 11cm (4½"), AUS $70-85; US $45-55; £30-35.

Above right: "Reid's Stout" James Green & Nephew, 15.5cm (6¼"), AUS $800-1000; US $525-625; £325-400.

Right: "Ross's Ginger Ale" Mintons, 9cm (3½"), AUS $500-600; US $300-350; £200-250.

Below left: "Red Label Liqueur Scotch" Shelley, 12.5cm (4¾"), AUS $1000-1250; US $600-750; £400-475.

Below right: "Royal Huntsman Scotch Whisky" stoneware, no base mark, 16.5cm (6½"), AUS $600-750; US $375-450; £250-300.

Above left: "Robertson's Yellow Label Scotch Whisky" Royal Staffordshire Pottery, 8cm (3″), AUS $450-500; US $300-350; £175-200.

Right: Glass back bar dispenser advertising "John Robertson & Son Scotch Whisky, Dundee" gold and red enamel print on body and top, 62cm (24½″) high, AUS $3500-4000; US $2250-2500; £1400-1600.

Below left: "Robertson's Scotch Whisky" no base mark, 10cm (4″), AUS $350-400; US $225-250; £125-150.

Below centre: "Robertson's Yellow Label Scotch Whisky" Wedekind & Co., London, 14cm (5½″), AUS $800-1000; US $500-650; £325-400.

Below right: "Robertson Dundee Whisky" ashtray, Wedekind & Co., London, 11.5cm (4½″) square, AUS $250-300; US $160-190; £100-120.

Above left: Honey amber glass decanter, "John Robertson & Son, Dundee - Fine Old Scotch Whisky" incised white enamelled print, overall 25cm (10″) high, incl. stopper. (original stopper would have been amber glass to match decanter). AUS $700-850; US $450-525; £275-325.
Above right: Emerald green glass decanter "Robertson's Dundee Whisky" enamelled white script, overall 23cm (9″) high, AUS $800-1000; US $500-650; £325-350.

Below left: "Robbie Burns Famed Old Scotch Whisky" HCW, 10cm (4″), AUS $150-180; US $100-120; £40-50. **Below right:** "Ross Brothers Whisky" no base mark, 18cm (7″), AUS $650-750; US $425-500; £250-300.

"Sandeman Scotch Whisky" no base mark, 11cm (4½″), AUS $140-175; US $90-110; £55-65.

"Sandeman Scotch Whisky" Made in England, 11.5cm (4½″), AUS $140-175; US $90-110; £55-65.

"Sandeman V.V.O. Scotch Whisky" Thorne Advertising Glasgow, 9cm (3½″), AUS $180-210; US $120-140; £70-80.

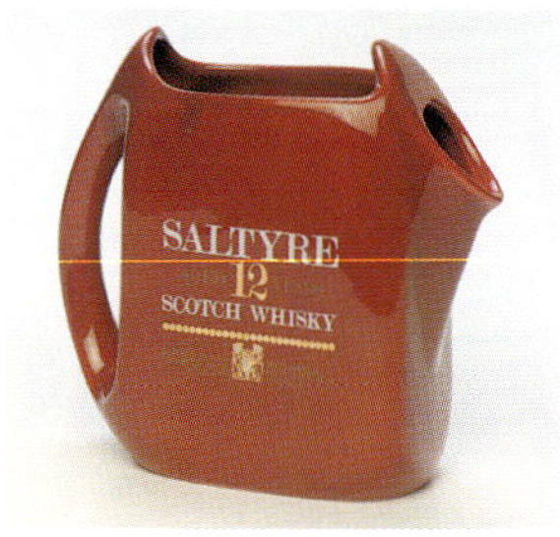

"Saltyre Scotch Whisky" Euroceramics, 15cm (6″), AUS $70-85; US $45-55; £25-30.

"The Silver Strand Scotch Whisky" no base mark, 11cm (4½″), AUS $70-85; US $45-55; £25-30.

"Scotia Royale 21 Year Old Scotch Whisky" miniature jug, Highland China, Scotland, 7cm (2¾″), AUS $90-110; US $45-55; £25-30.

"Seagram's 100 Pipers De Luxe Scotch Whisky" San Claudio, 20cm (8″), AUS $75-90; US $50-60; £30-35.

"Sykes Crown Vat" Wade, 14cm (5½″), AUS $180-210; US $110-130; £70-80.

"Scottish Islay Liqueur, Malt Whisky" miniature jug, 8cm (3″), AUS $65-75; US $40-50; £25-30.

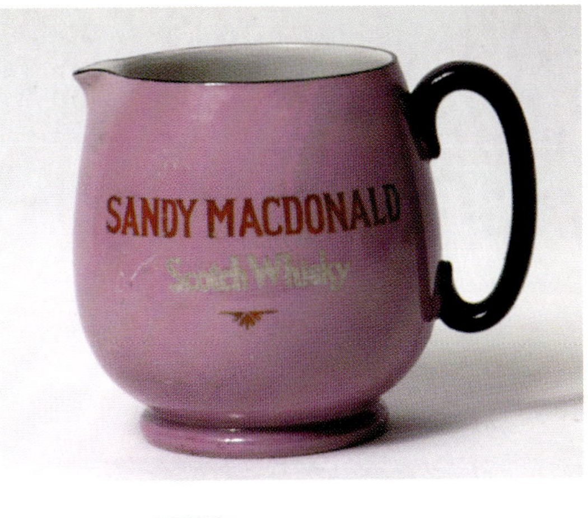

Above: "Sandy Macdonald Scotch Whisky" glass decanter, 26cm (10¼″) high, AUS $250-300; US $160-190; £100-125. **Above right:** "Sandy Macdonald Scotch Whisky" Made in England, 11cm (4½″), AUS $350-400; US $225-250; £140-165. **Middle left:** "Seagram's VO Canadian Whisky" pewter, 18cm (7″), AUS $100-125; US $65-75; £40-50. **Middle right:** "Seagram's VO Canadian Whisky" no base mark, 13cm (5″), AUS $75-90; US $45-55; £30-35. **Right:** "Stromness Scotch Whisky" glass decanter, three dimples, 24cm (9½″), AUS $200-250; US $125-150; £100-120. **Below:** "Stewart's Dundee De Luxe Scotch Whisky" Wade Regicor, 9.5cm (3¾″), AUS $200-225; US $125-150; £75-85.

Above: **Above:** "Squires Gin" ceramic figure, 24cm (9¼"), AUS $500-600; US $325-365; £200-250.

Above: "Slemish Liqueur Whisky" J.A. Campbell, Belfast, 7.5cm (2¾"), AUS $400-450; US $250-300; £160-190.

Above: "Simpson Shepherd & Sons Fortification Scotch Whisky" Aberdeen, 9.5cm (3¾"), AUS $400-450; US $250-300; £160-190.

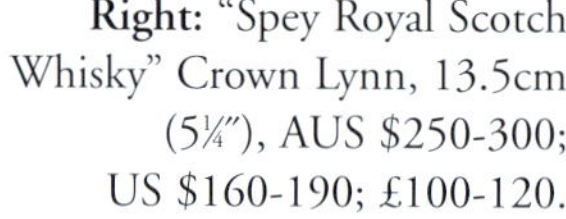

Right: "Spey Royal Scotch Whisky" Crown Lynn, 13.5cm (5¼"), AUS $250-300; US $160-190; £100-120.

Above left: "Stuart Royal Liqueur Whisky" stoneware jug, no base mark, 12.5cm ((4¾"), AUS $1000-1250; US $650-750; £400-500. **Above centre:** "J & C Stewart's Whisky" ashtray, Fielding & Co, Stoke-On-Trent, 13 x 10cm (5 x 4"), AUS $250-300; US $150-175; £100-120. **Above right:** "Suntory Whisky" Buchan Portobello, 16.5cm (6½"), AUS $70-90; US $45-55; £25-30.

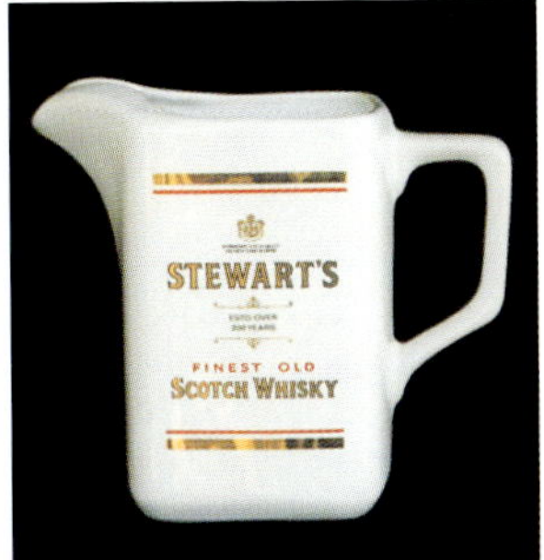

Above left: "House Of Stuart Blended Scotch Whisky" HCW, 12cm (4¾"), AUS $190-220; US $120-140; £75-90 **Above centre:** "Stewart's Finest Old Scotch Whisky" no base mark, 15cm (6"), AUS $90-110; US $60-70; £35-40. **Above right:** "Jamie Stuart Scotch Whisky" Wade Regicor, 14cm (5½"), AUS $170-200; US $100-120; £65-75.

Below left: "Springbank Scotch Whisky" Wade, 16cm (6¼"), AUS $135- 165; US $85-95; £50-60. **Below centre:** "Springbank Scotch Whisky" Highland China, 16cm (6¼"), AUS $80-100; US $50-60; £30-35. **Below right:** "Springbank Scotch Whisky" Wade PDM, 18.5cm (7¼"), AUS $120-140; US $75-85; £45-50.

Right: Plastic Peg Leg Pirate figure advertising "More Hops In Ben Truman" Ales, height 49.5cm (17½"), AUS $500-600; US $300-350; £200-225.

Middle: "Truman's Ales And Stout" Mintons, 14cm (5½"), AUS $350- 400; US $225-255; £140-160.

Bottom left: "Train & McIntyre V.O. Red Seal Whisky" no base mark, 12.5cm (4¾"), AUS $550-650; US $350-400; £220-250.

Bottom right: Brown top stoneware jug advertising "Drink Toohey's Ales" no base mark, 16.5cm (6¼"), AUS $700-850; US $450-550; £275-325.

TEACHER'S

The right spirit boys!

Teachers "The Right Spirit Boys"

An opportunist photograph, taken in a London street nearly 70 years ago, led to lifetime financial support for two little boys, plus one of Teacher's most famous advertising campaigns.

A Sunday Pictorial photographer came across two little ragamuffins having fun playing cricket - using a battered old cricket bat and three empty bottles for the wicket as he went about his business back in 1926, and astutely decided to capture the incident on film.

As it turned out the bottles, or wickets, had been rescued from the nearest rubbish bin and comprised two unlabelled glass bottles and an empty Teacher's whisky bottle.

When the photo appeared, Teacher's directors immediately realised the potential commercial viability of the appealing snap, and purchased it from the photographer.

The result was that the photograph became the main theme of Teacher's advertising and promotional activity throughout the early 1930's and became extremely successful.

Indeed some in the industry have suggested that Teacher's should re-run some of the advertising executions today, for nostalgia's sake. However one leading advertising industry analyst said: "It was a clever campaign of its time, but it could not be done today because of the problems of linking whisky with children."

New details of this intriguing story have emerged from a series of letters found in the dusty archives during the recent move from Teacher's Glasgow headquarters in St. Enoch Square to Dumbarton.

Being a family business of strong social conscience, typical of most Scottish businessmen, Teacher's were keen to contact the stars of the photograph and suitably reward them.

Set of three jugs featuring Frank and Charlie, the Right Spirit Boys produced during the late 1920s to promote "Teacher's Scotch Whisky."

From left: Base marked Made in Engalnd, 8cm (3"), AUS $250-300; US $160-190; £100-120.

Centre: Also made in England, 9.5cm (3¾"), AUS $250-300; US $160-190; £100-120.

Right: Tillstone Ware Providence Pottery, 15.5cm (6"), scarcest of the three sizes, AUS $600-700; US $400-450; £240-280.

The boys, who had by this time been christened "The Right Spirit Boys" were traced to the Smith family in London's Brixton area. The elder boy, Charlie, was six years old, and the younger, Frank, was four.

The old files reveal that an annual allowance of £5 for each boy - a veritable fortune in those days - was paid to Mrs Smith from the Teacher's directors to help in bringing up her boys.

In one of the annual letters, dated June 22, 1939 - just before World War Two - a Teacher's director wrote: "We take pleasure again in sending you £10 which we hope will enable you to take a holiday with your family." The £10 in those days would have been more than enough for a holiday, when the price of a bottle of Teacher's Highland Cream retailed at around three shillings and sixpence.

The correspondence is a fascinating history lesson. A 1940 letter revealed Frank had just celebrated his 18th birthday while her younger children had been evacuated to Sussex for safety during the war. In 1941 one of the Right Spirit Boys was in the army, the other in the RAF.

In October, 1942 Charlie was moved to Scotland and stationed at Ayr. He wrote to his benefactors in St. Enoch Square to arrange a meeting. "I have passed your offices many times, and never plucked up the courage to come in." Naturally, the Teacher's directors were delighted to see Charlie when he finally called.

The next year Charlie was sent abroad to serve in Italy and became a father when his wife gave birth to a baby girl.

In 1945 Teacher's sent one of their London based representatives to see Mrs Smith. Now aged 60, she earned thirty shillings (£1.50 in today's coinage) a week from her cleaning job, plus a widow's pension of ten shillings (50p) and an allowance of seven shillings (35p) from one of her sons in the army. With a total weekly income of £2.35 the allowance from Teacher's was well received.

By 1947 both the Right Spirit Boys were married. Charlie had settled in Ayr with his family, working as a welder, and Frank was in London. Charlie and his family emigrated to America in 1949, while Frank found work in the building trade, becoming the father of twins the next year. Sadly Charlie was killed in 1951 in an accident at work in New York.

By 1957 Mrs Smith had 21 grandchildren, but her bronchitis was causing her problems. By 1962, at the age of 76, her daughter was living with her as she was unable to manage on her own.

In 1964 Mrs Smith was rehoused in a charming little flat. Her only complaint was the rent, which had more than quadrupled from thirteen shillings (65p) to two pounds and eighteen shillings (£2.90) a week.

Frank sadly died from cancer in 1967 at the age of 43, but Teacher's continued the annual calls on Mrs Smith and sending flowers when she was ill – to ensure that the annual allowance arrived safely until she died in December 1978 at the age of 92.

Little did the photographer know that one picture, taken in 1926, would lead to this amazing lifelong relationship between one of the world's leading and most respected blended whiskies and a struggling family from London's Brixton area.

Tin calendar "make a date with a teacher" 24 x 17cm (9½ x 6¾"),
AUS $125-150; US $80-100; £50-60.

Right: Two rubber compound bar figures advertising "Teacher's Scotch Whisky." The figure on left is 35cm (14") high, AUS $1000-1250; US $650- 800; £400-500. The figure on right is not as rare 30cm (12") high, AUS $650-800; US $425-475; £275-325.

Below left: "Teacher's Highland Cream" James Green & Nephew, 9cm (3½"), AUS $650-750; US $425-500; £250-300.

Below right: "Teacher's Scotch Whisky" ceramic plate, back stamped with distiller's name, 25.5cm (10") dia, AUS $125-150; US $80-100; £50-60.

Right: Teacher's Highland Cream Scotch Whisky" rubber compound bar figure on wooden base, 36cm (14″) high, AUS $800-1000; US $500-650; £325- 400.

The jug in the photograph is the smallest in a series of three, 8cm (3¼″) high, distillers name on base, AUS $ 175-200; US $ 110-130; £70-80.

Bottom: Pair of jugs titled "Teacher's Highland Cream Scotch Whisky" the left jug features a scene of the distillery while the right jug features a scene of scotsmen toasting John Barleycorn with verse by Robert Burns. Both Seton Pottery, 16cm (6¼″) high, AUS $125-150; US $80-95; £50-60 each.

Above left: "Teacher's Scotch Whisky, A Measure Of Character" Seton, 16cm (6¼″), AUS $80-95; US $50-60; £30-35. **Above centre:** "Teacher's Highland Cream Scotch Whisky" Highland China, Scotland, 16cm (6¼″), AUS $75-90; US $50-60; £30-35. **Above right:** "Teacher's Highland Cream" Piola, 15cm (6″), AUS $75- 90; US $50-60; £30-35.

Above left: "Tamnavulin Single Malt Scotch Whisky, Glenlivet" HCW, 9cm (3½″), AUS $125-150; US $80-100; £50-60. **Above centre:** "Teacher's Highland Cream Whisky" matchstriker, S. Fielding, 10cm (4″) dia, AUS $175-225; US $110-130; £70-85. **Above right:** "A.G. Thomson & Co.'s Scotch Whiskies" brass ashtray, 12cm (4¾″) dia, AUS $45-55; US $30-40; £20-25

Below: "Teacher's Highland Cream Scotch Whisky" Seton, 16cm (6¼″), AUS $90-120; US $60-70; £35-40. **Below right:** "Tullamore Dew Liqueur Whisky" Arklow, 11.5cm (4½″), AUS $400-450; US $250-300; £150-170.

Above: "Teacher's Highland Cream" Piola, 10cm (4″), AUS $90-110; US $55-65; £35-40.

Above top left: "Teacher's Highland Cream" Piola, 13cm (5″), AUS $90-110; US $55-65; £35-40. **Above left:** Glass flask in leather case titled "Teachers" 15cm (6″) high, AUS $140-180; US $90-110; £50-60. **Above centre:** "Teacher's Highland Cream Whisky" glass decanter, 25cm (10½″) high, AUS $250-300; US $150-175; £100-120. **Above right:** "Teacher's Scotch Whisky" ceramic plate, distillers name on back, 25.5cm (10″) dia, AUS $125-150; US $80-95; £50-60.

Below: Two bulbous bodied white jugs titled "Teacher" distiller's name on base, largest 13cm (5″) high, smallest 8cm (3¼″) high. These were produced in three sizes, below are largest and smallest in the set, all valued at AUS $175-200; US $110-130; £70-80 each.

Appealing Victorian tin display sign advertising "Turnbull's Standard Extra Special Scotch Whisky" circa 1900, 46 x 32cm (18 x 12½"), AUS $300-350; US $200-230; £120-140.

Above: Glass decanter "Thorne's Choicest Scotch Whisky" 25cm (10″) high, AUS $400-500; US $250-325; £160-200.

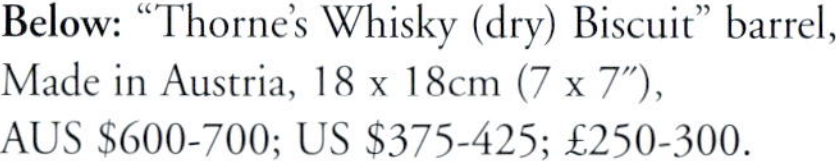

Below: "Thorne's Whisky (dry) Biscuit" barrel, Made in Austria, 18 x 18cm (7 x 7″), AUS $600-700; US $375-425; £250-300.

Above: "Thorne's Scotch" Wade Regicor, 17cm (6¾″), AUS $200-250; US $130-160; £80-100.

Below: "Thorne's Scotch Whisky" Royal Doulton, 20cm (8″), AUS $800- 1000; US $500-600; £325-375.

Right: Magnificent "Thorne's Whisky" floral decanter, Copeland Late Spode, 27cm (10½") high, AUS $700-900; US $450-550; £300-350.

Below left: "Thorne's Scotch Whisky" match-holder, Doulton Lambeth, 8cm (3¼"), AUS $425-500; US $260-300; £160-185.

Below right: "Thorne's - The Best Whisky" matchstriker, Royal Doulton, 8 x 8cm (3 x 3"), AUS $500-600; US $325-375; £200-230.

Right: "Thorne's Whisky" matchstriker, Dutch manufacture, 13cm (5") dia, AUS $400-450; US $250-280; £160-180.

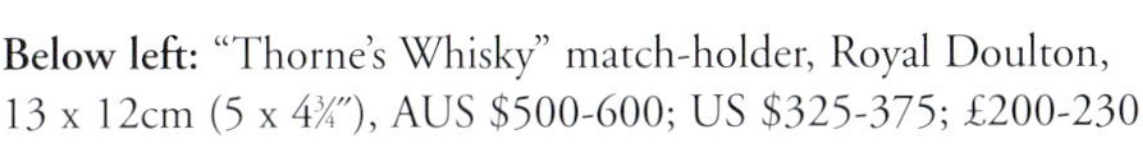

Below left: "Thorne's Whisky" match-holder, Royal Doulton, 13 x 12cm (5 x 4¾"), AUS $500-600; US $325-375; £200-230.

Below centre: "Thorne's Whisky" matchstriker, no base stamp, 13 x 12cm (5 x 4¾"), AUS $450-500; US $275-300; £175-200.

Below right: "Thorne's Whisky" matchstriker, Royal Doulton, 12cm (4¾") high, AUS $500-600; US $325-375; £200-250.

Above left: "Usher's Green Stripe Whisky" (dry) biscuit barrel without lid, James Green & Nephew, 16cm (6¼″), AUS $400-500; US $250-300; £160-190. **Above right:** "Usher's Green Stripe Whisky" Shelly, 16cm (6¼″), AUS $750-850; US $500-600; £300-350.

Right: "Vat 69 - Sanderson's Liqueur Scotch Whisky" ashbowl, James Green & Nephew, 10 x 4.5cm (4 x 1¾″), AUS $125-150; US $80-95; £50-60.

Below: "Usher's Whisky" water carafe, 20cm (8″), AUS $175-225; US $110-140; £70-85.

Below: "Usher's O.V.G Whisky" match-holder, Raphael Tuck & Sons, London, 6.5 x 9cm (2½ x 3½″), AUS $150-180; US $100-120; £60- 70.

Above top: "Usher's Green Stripe Scotch Whisky" glass ashtray, 10.5cm (4¼") dia, AUS $150-175; US $100-120; £60-70.

Above: "Usher's O.V.G. Scotch Whisky" glass ashtray, 10.5cm (4¼") dia, AUS $150-175; US $100-120; £60-70.

Above: "Usher's Green Stripe Scotch" plaster figure, 42cm (16½"), AUS $1000-1250; US $650-800; £400-500.

Below left: "Vat 69 - The Scotch Whisky" Contesa, Spain, 13cm (5"), AUS $130-150; US $80-90; £50-60. **Below centre:** "Vat 69 Gold Classic Light" base stamped with U.S. Importer's name, 14cm (5½"), AUS $110-130; US $60-75; £40-50. **Below right:** "Vat 69 Scotch Whisky" HCW, 18cm (7"), AUS $140-170; US $90-110; £55-65.

Johnnie Walker

The original John Walker began his career as a grocer in Kilmarnock. Whisky making was a sideline which gradually took over until the grocery shop became a wine and spirit business.

It was thirty years until his son Alexander saw the advantages of wholesale over retail and the Walker whisky blend made its first appearance on the wholesale market.

The Walkers began supplying whisky to the ships sailing out of Glasgow. As a centre for carpet making Kilmarnock brought a steady stream of business to the town and so the reputation of Walker's Kilmarnock whisky grew.

Alexander's sons joined the business and upon his death the youngest, Alex, was appointed head of the organisation.

The family business had offices in London and in 1890 Alec's brother John travelled to Australia to continue the company's expansion. Until 1939 Australia was the main overseas' market for Walker's Scotch whisky.

When John died another Walker took his place nurturing the product's success. Between 1880 and 1897 Walker's whisky won awards in Sydney, Melbourne, Adelaide, Brisbane and Dunedin – achievements still noted on the Red Label bottle.

In 1908 the distinctive Johnnie Walker title and square bottle appeared on the market. The image of Johnnie Walker in full stride along with the slogan "Johnnie Walker, born 1820 – still going strong" appeared later and has endured since.

More than ten years earlier the Walkers had moved their distilling operations up stream after acquiring Cardow. While maintaining a small interest in pot-still malt distilling, Walker's continued expanding their blending and exporting activities.

Left: A postcard advertising "Johnnie Walker" dated 1926.

Under the control of James Stevenson the company became the largest blenders and bottlers of Scotch whisky in the world.

In 1925 Walker's merged with Buchanan-Dewar and DCL. Since that day the company had maintained its trading independency and growth.

Today Johnnie Walker Red Label remains the most popular Scotch on the market with Johnnie Walker Black Label considered the deluxe alternative.

One in every six bottles of Scotch whisky exported is Johnnie Walker with the USA representing the biggest market.

Other brands include Cardhu 12 year old Highland Malt, Old Harmony and Swing, sometimes known as Celebrity.

Above right: "Johnnie Walker Scotch Whisky" plaster compound figure, 39cm (15½") high, AUS $500-600; US $300-360; £200-240.

Below left: "Johnnie Walker" Elischer, Aust., 16cm (6½"), AUS $300-400; US $200-250; £120-150.
Below centre: "Johnnie Walker" Elischer, Aust., 12cm (4¾"), AUS $250-300; US $160-200; £100-120.
Below right: "Johnnie Walker" Elischer, Aust., 16cm (6¼"), AUS $95-110; US $60-70; £40-50.

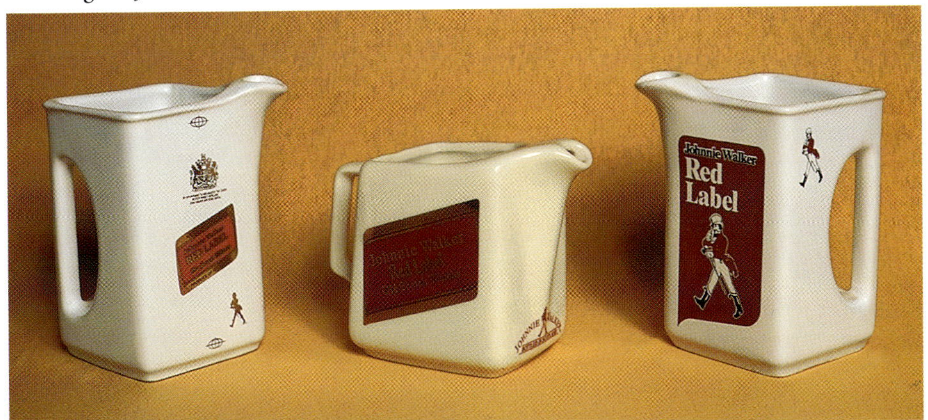

Above: Descriptions and values on facing page.

Left: Series of four jugs produced recently advertising "Johnnie Walker" Scotch Whisky featuring oval coloured sporting scenes of Johnnie as follows:
(1) "Curling" (2) "Golfing" (3) "Skating" and (4) "Coaching." All 16cm (6¼") high, Made in England, AUS $90-120; US $50- 60; £25-30.

Opposite page: Selection of bar figures advertising Johnnie Walker Scotch Whisky. The four larger figures are all approx. 40cm (15½″) high. Three of these are plaster compound on wooden base, their values range between AUS $500-700; US $325-425; £200-250 depending on condition. The large centre figure with bright red coat is made from an early type of plastic and is valued at AUS $800-1000; US $500-600; £325-400. The half size 18cm (7″) figure is also plaster compound, valued at AUS $350-400; US $225-265; £140- 165. The miniature figure is plastic, valued at AUS $140-175; US $90-110; £55-65.

Above: "Walker's Kilmarnock Whisky" James Green & Nephew, 16cm (6¼″) high, AUS $550-650; US $365-425; £220-260.

Above: Johnnie Walker change tray, Wade Regicor, 26 x 15cm (10 x 6″), AUS $70-85; US $45-55; £28-35

Below: "Johnnie Walker Scotch Whisky" tin calendar, 23 x 29cm (9 x 11½″), AUS $600-700; US $400-450; £250-280.

Above left: "Johnnie Walker Red" base stamped with U.S. Importer's name, 13cm (5″), AUS $200-250; US $130-160; £80-100. **Above centre:** "Johnnie Walker Whisky" leather dice shaker, Made in England, 9.5cm (3¾″), AUS $80-100; US $50-65; £30-40. **Above right:** "Johnnie Walker" copper ashtray, 14.5 x 10.5cm (5¼ x 4″), AUS $80-100; US $50-60; £30-35. **Right:** "Johnnie Walker" spelter matchstriker, 15cm (6″) high, AUS $600-750; US $375-450; £250-300. **Below left:** Milk glass figural decanter depicting Johnnie Walker, handpainted, 28cm (11″) high with plastic hat. AUS $90-120; US $60-75; £35-45. **Below centre:** Small "Johnnie Walker" figure, 15cm (6″) high overall, AUS $450-525; US $300-350; £180-210. **Below right:** "Johnnie Walker" free-standing tin plate figure, 25cm (10″) high, AUS $225-275; US $140-170; £90-110.

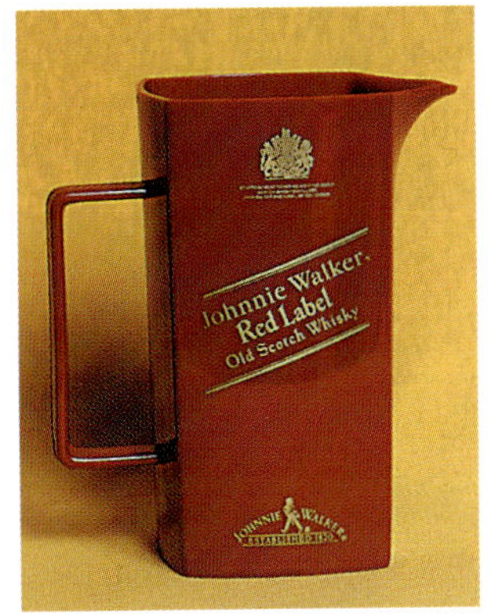

Above left: "Johnnie Walker Red Label" Wade, 19cm (7½"), AUS $125-150; US $80-95; £50-60.

Above centre: "Johnnie Walker Red Label" plastic jug, Monza Italy, 16cm (6¼"), AUS $45-55; US $30-40; £20-25.

Above right: "Johnnie Walker" Wade, 16.5cm (6¼"), AUS $300-350; US $200-240; £120-140.

Right: "Johnnie Walker Scotch Whisky" tin calendar, 24 x 23cm (9½ x 9"), AUS $130-160; US $85-105; £50-60.

Below left & right: Two different "Johnnie Walker" jugs, bases stamped Gleneagles 63, 13cm (5") high, AUS $300-350; US $200-230; £120-140 each.

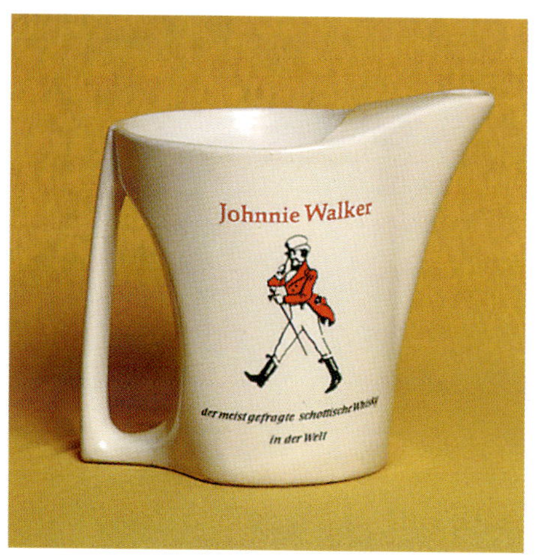

Above left: "Johnnie Walker" no base mark, German jug, 11.75cm (4¾"), AUS $200-250; US $125-155; £80-100. **Above right:** "Johnnie Walker Red Label" Moulin Des Loups, 14cm (5½"), AUS $500-600; US $300-350; £200-225.

Above left: Johnnie Walker figure only, no title, Amberglade, 13.5cm (5¼"), AUS $90-110; US $55-65; £35-40. **Above centre:** "Johnnie Walker" ashtray, James Green & Nephew, 12cm (4¾"), AUS $350-400; US $225-255; £140-165. **Above right:** "Johnnie Walker" Royal Doulton, 16cm (6¼"), AUS $1000-1250; US $650-800; £400-500.

Below left: "Johnnie Walker" Made in England, 18cm (7"), AUS $85- 100; US $45-55; £25-30. **Below centre:** "Johnnie Walker" Staffordshire Pottery, 13cm (5¼"), AUS $350-400; US $225-255; £140-165. **Below right:** "Johnnie Walker" James Green & Nephew, 12cm (4¾"), AUS $400-450; US $245-275; £150-175.

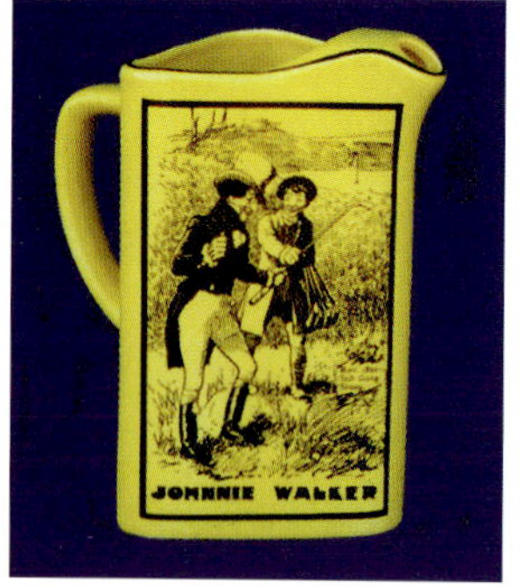

Attractive tin serving tray advertising "Johnnie Walker" Scotch Whisky, 40 x 30cm (16 x 12"), AUS $500-650; US $325-375; £200-250.

Above left: "Johnnie Walker Black Label Old Scotch Whisky" Piola, Italy, 15cm (6″), AUS $175-200; US $110-130; £70-80. **Above right:** "Johnnie Walker" menu holder, 7cm (2¾″) high, AUS $220- 250; US $140-160; £80-90.

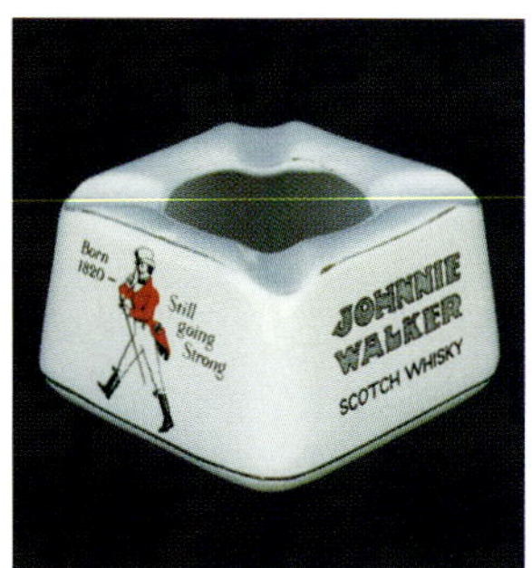

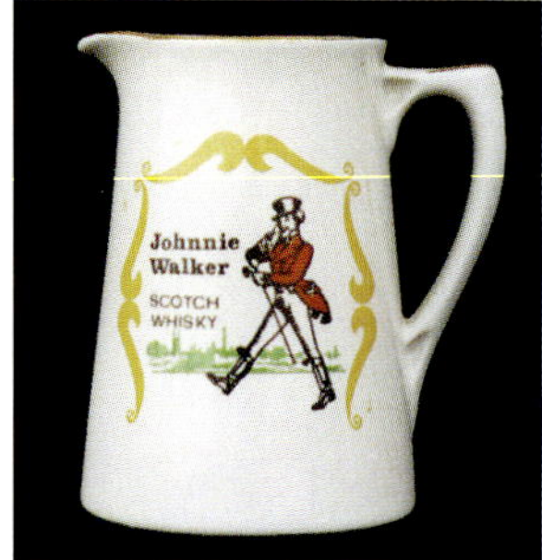

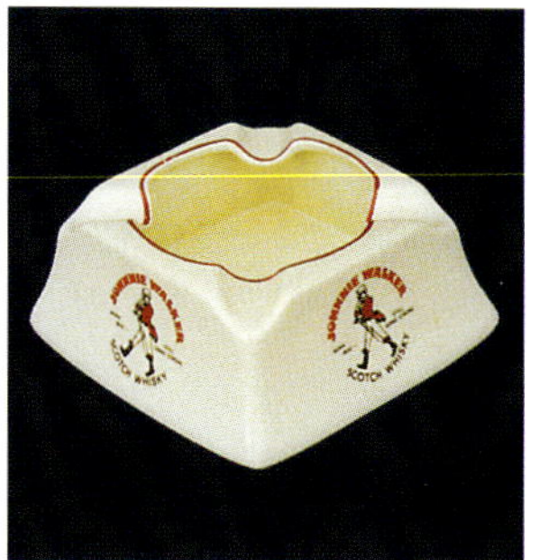

Above left: "Johnnie Walker Scotch Whisky" ashbowl, James Green & Nephew, 10.5cm (4″) square, AUS $100-130; US $65-80; £40-50. **Above centre:** "Johnnie Walker Scotch Whisky" Made in England, 11cm (4¼″), AUS $220-250; US $140-165; £85-95. **Above right:** "Johnnie Walker Scotch Whisky" ashbowl, Wade Regicor, 12cm (4¾″) square, AUS $110-130; US $70-85; £45-55.

Below left: "Johnnie Walker Red Label Old Scotch Whisky" ashtray, Wade PDM, 16.5cm (6½″) square, AUS $55-70; US $35-45; £20-25. **Below centre:** "Johnnie Walker" paper wrapped carton containing 20 boxes of matches, full carton AUS $125-150; US $80-95; £50-60, single packet AUS $12-15; US $8-10; £4-5. **Below right:** "Johnnie Walker Scotch Whisky" ashtray, James Green & Nephew, 13.5cm (5¼″) square, AUS $125-150; US $80-95; £50-60.

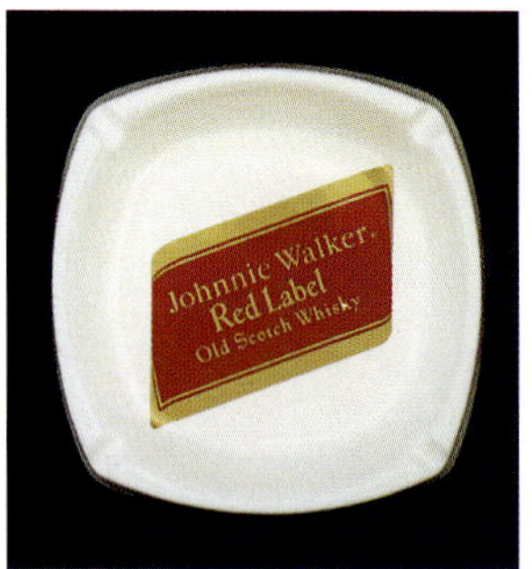

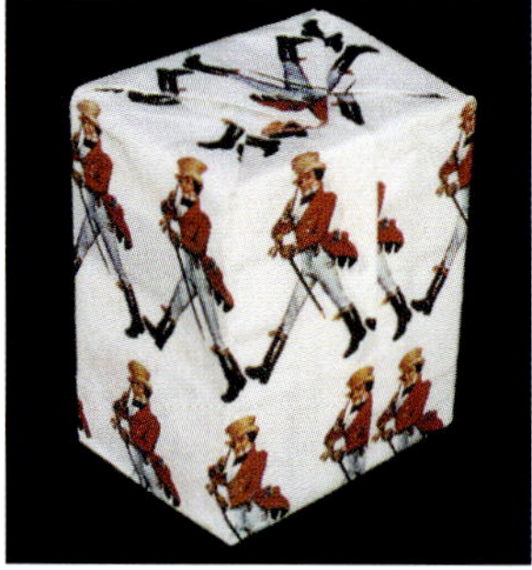

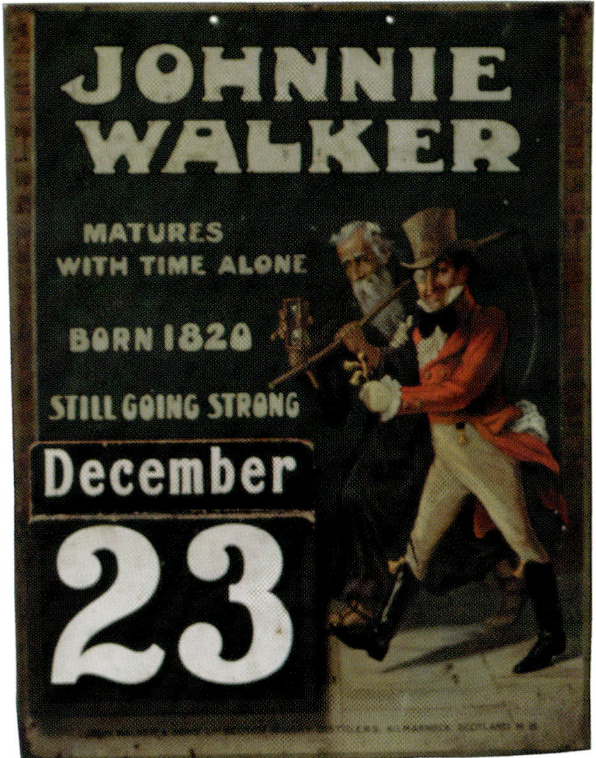

Right: "Johnnie Walker Matures with Time Alone" tin calendar, 43 x 33cm (17 x 13″), AUS $1000-1250; US $650-800; £400-500.

Below: "Johnnie Walker Classic" no base mark, 12cm (4¾″), AUS $250-300; US $160-190; £100-120.

Below: Two rare yellow "Johnnie Walker - You'll Find Him Everywhere" jugs, James Green & Nephew, left 12cm (4¾″) high, right 15cm (6″) high, both valued at AUS $1750-2000; US $1100-1250; £700-800.

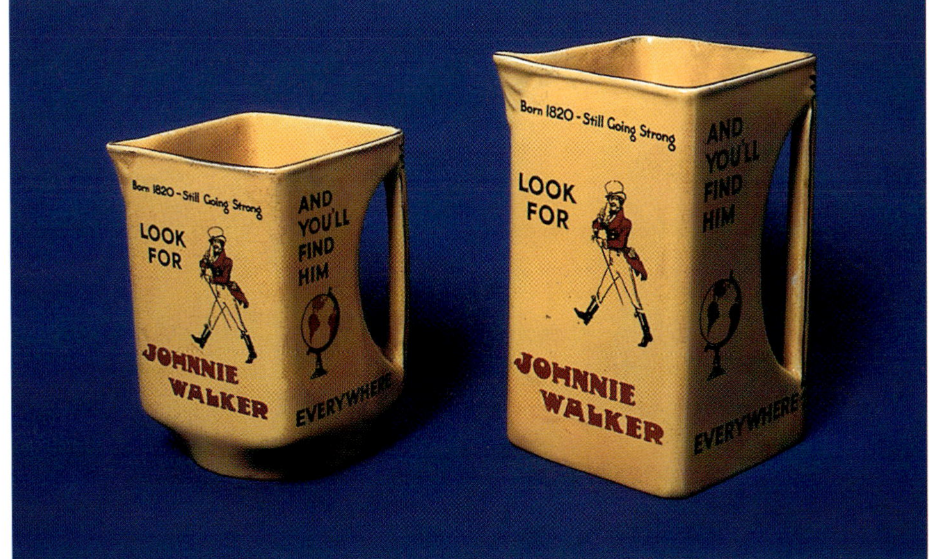

Above: Johnnie Walker print on canvas, wooden frame, 59 x 50cm (23 x 19½"), circa 1973, AUS $400-450; US $250-300; £150-180.

Below: "Johnnie Walker Bridge Score" book hard cover, 22 x 9.5cm (8½ x 3¾"), 80 pages, AUS $50-65; US $30-40; £20-25.

Below left: "Johnnie Walker Scotch Whisky" plastic ice bucket, Marquis Australia, 20cm (8") high, AUS $60-75; US $35-45; £25-30. **Below centre:** "Born 1820, Still Going Strong" porcelain spirit measure, 13cm (5") in length, produced in many different styles, this one is scarce, AUS $70-85; US $45-55; £25-30. **Below right:** "Johnnie Walker" tin calendar, 28 x 23.5cm (11 x 9¼"), AUS $135-165; US $80-105; £50-65.

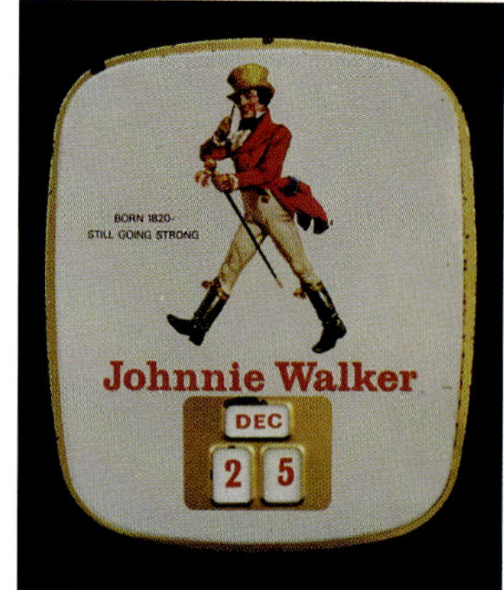

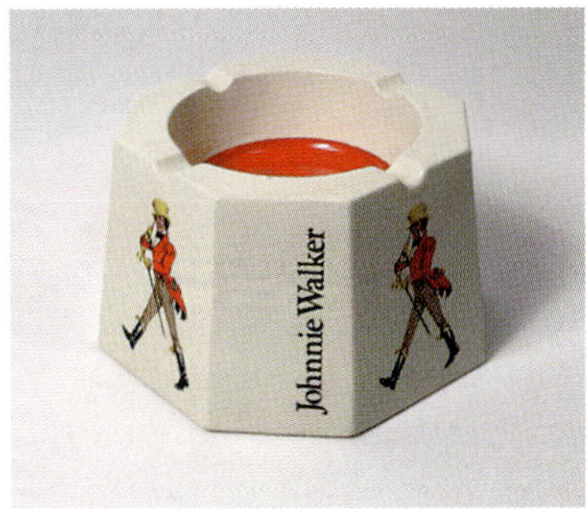

Above: "Johnnie Walker" ceramic ashbowl, no base mark, 21cm (8¼") dia x 13.5cm (5¼") high, circa 1960, rare, AUS $600-700; US $350-400; £225-250.

Right: "Johnnie Walker" celluloid covered tin sign, 70 x 47cm (28 x 18½"), AUS $400-500; US $250-300; £150-175.

"Johnnie Walker" matchstriker, James Green & Nephew, 13cm (5") dia, AUS $500-575; US $325-375; £200-230.

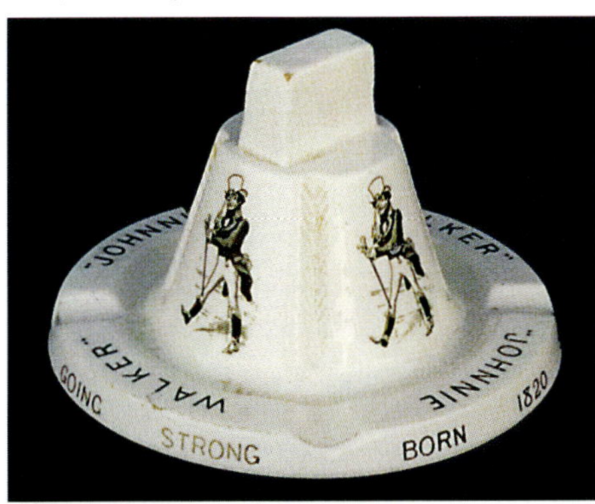

"Johnnie Walker" copper serving tray, 34cm (13½") dia, AUS $130-170; US $85-105; £50-60.

Watson's

Some of the most aspiring whisky collectables were produced to advertise Watson's whisky and although few records are available we do know that James Watson & Co. Ltd. was established in Dundee in 1815 as a blender and marketer of whisky.

Watson's purchased three distilleries during the latter part of the nineteenth century, the first being the Ord Distillery in 1897. Watson's acquired the Parkmore Distillery in 1900 and the Pulteney Distillery in 1920.

Production of whisky was suspended during the First World War as the cereals normally used for whisky were redirected to the war effort. Watson's were unable to recover from this slump in production and in 1923 were taken over by a combination of Buchanans, Dewars and Johnnie Walker. The eight million gallons of whisky which Watson's had in storage was divided by new owners Buchanans and Johnnie Walker.

The high quality of Watson's advertising can be assessed from the few examples appearing on these pages.

Below: "Watson's No. 10 Scotch Whisky" ceramic serving tray, no base stamp, 26.5 x 24cm (10½ x 9½"), AUS $300-350; US $175-200; £120-140.

Below left: "Watson's Dundee Whisky" match-holder, no base stamp, 7 x 9cm (2¾ x 3½"), AUS $400-450; US $260-300; £160-180.

Below centre: "Watson's No. 10 Scotch" Minton, England, 11cm (4½"), AUS $300-350; US $180-220; £120-140.

Below right: "Watson's No. 10 Scotch" ashtray, Minton, England, 10 x 14cm (4 x 5½"), AUS $140-165; US $90-110; £55-65.

Right: "Watson's No.10 Scotch Whisky" change tray, no base stamp, 16cm (6¼″) dia, AUS $400-500; US $250-300; £160-200.

Below: "Watson's Dundee Whisky" matchstriker, 11.5cm (4½″) dia, AUS $170-200; US $110-130; £65-75.

Below: Two different ruby glass decanters advertising "Watson's" Scotch Whisky in white enamelled print, circa 1900, both have applied clear glass handles, ground glass stoppers, 23cm (9″) high overall, exceptionally rare, AUS $1500-2000; US $1000-1250; £600-800 each.

Above: "Watson's No. 10 Scotch" matchbox holder/ashtray, Shelley (distiller's name on base), 11.5 X 7cm (4½ x 2¾"), AUS $300-350; US $180-210; £120-140.

Left: "Watson's Scotch" Wileman – Foley Intarsio England, 22cm (8½") high, rare, AUS $3000-3500; US $2000-2300; £1200-1400.

Opposite page centre: "Watson's No. 10" Scotch Whisky pewter jug, Walker & Hall, Sheffield, England, 18cm (7"), AUS $300-350; US $190-220; £120-140.

Below: Two different Shelley (late Foley) decanters advertising "Watson's Scotch" 21.5cm (8½") high, rare, AUS $3250-3750; US $2000-2500; £1300-1500 each.

Above: "Watson's No. 10 Scotch" ashbowl, Shelley (no base stamp), 11cm (4½″) dia, AUS $125-150; US $80-95; £50-60.

Right: Glass back bar dispenser advertising "Watson's Three Stars Scotch Whisky" in gold recessed paint, brass tap, overall 72cm (28½″) high, AUS $2500-3000; US $1600-1900; £1000-1250.

Below: "Watson's Blue Band" match-holder/ashtray, no base mark but obviously Shelley, 14.5 x 10cm (5½ x 4″), AUS $400-500; US $260-300; £160-180.

White Horse

White Horse Distillers Ltd takes its name from one of the company's most successful brands, White Horse Cellar Scotch Whisky.

The company was originally known as Mackie and Company Distillers Ltd until the death of Sir Peter Mackie in 1924 when the White Horse title was adopted.

Marketing was the key to Mackie's success. He realised the potential of the international market and the need to supply a high quality product.

He chose the White Horse name because of the location of his ancestral home – near the White Horse Inn in the Canongate, Edinburgh. The Inn was already well known as a meeting place for writers and actors. The Edinburgh – London stagecoach also began its journey there.

Mackie's uncle had been in the whisky business and in time he inherited the Lagavulin distillery. He built a new distillery at Craigllachie in partnership with Alexander Edward. Mackie eventually took over the operation.

The company is now a subsidiary of DCL. As such it owns and operates Glen Elgin distillery in the parish of Longmorn.

The White Horse blending and bottling facility is located alongside another DCL controlled distillery, Port Dundas Grain Distillery.

Left: "White Horse Scotch Whisky" plaster figure, hollow inside top of hat to hold a standard size bottle of White Horse Whisky, figure itself is 24cm (9½″) high, AUS $700-900; US $450-550; £275-350.

Right: "White Horse Scotch Whisky" tin serving tray titled "Scotch Sampling in the Early Days" 30cm (12″) dia, AUS $200-250; US $130-160; £80-100.

Above: "White Horse Scotch" aluminium jug, 12cm (4¾″) high, AUS $110-130; US $70-80; £40-50.

Right: "White Horse Cellar" no base stamp, 18.5cm (7¼″), AUS $1000-1250; US $650-800; £400-500.

Left: "White Horse" no base stamp, 17cm (6¾″), AUS $85-100; US $55-65; £35-40.

Below right: Magnificent "Mackie's White Horse Cellar" ruby glass jug titled in white enamelled print with pictorial trademark, 15cm (6″) high, AUS $1500-2000; US $1000-1300; £600-800.

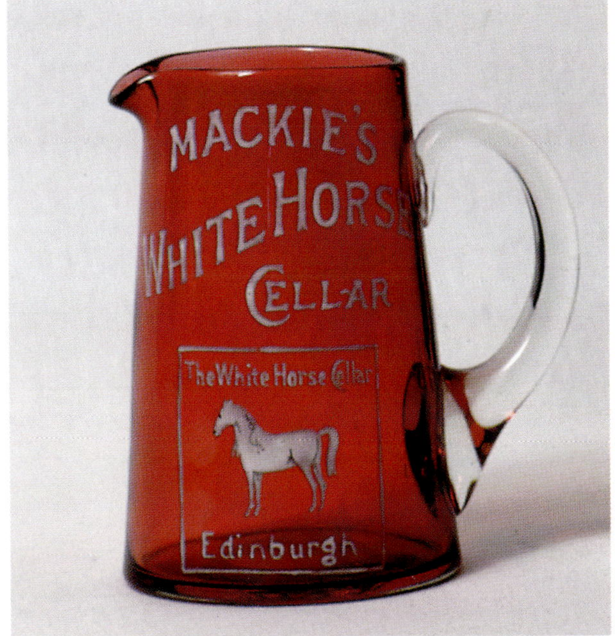

Below: "White Horse" match-striker, Shelley - Late Foley, 11.5cm (4½″) dia, AUS $400-450; US $250-300; £150-175.

Top right: "White Horse Whisky" ashtray, Shelley - Late Foley, 12.5 x 10cm (5 x 4″), AUS $250-300; US $150-175; £100-120.

Above: "White Horse Whisky" plaster compound figure, 24cm (9½″) high, AUS $300-350; US $200-230; £120-140.

Left: "White Horse Whisky" glass jug, 14cm (5½″), AUS $175-200; US $100-130; £70-85.

Below left: "White Horse Whisky" Fielding, 11cm (4½″) high, AUS $1500-1800; US $900-1100; £600-750. **Below right:** "White Horse Whisky" Shelley - Late Foley, 12.5cm (5″) high, AUS $400-500; US $250-300; £160-180.

Above left: "White Horse Scotch Whisky" wooden cased set of three glasses and bottle, glasses are 10cm (4″) high, AUS $250-325; US $150-200; £100-120. **Above right:** "White Horse" glass bottle in leather case, 28cm (11″) high, AUS $130-160; US $85-100; £50-60.

Right: "White Horse Fine Old Scotch Whisky" plastic figure, 25cm (10″) high, AUS $80-100; US $50-65; £30-40.

Far right: "White Horse Scotch Whisky" plastic figure, 13cm (5¼″) high, AUS $65-85; US $40-50; £25-30.

Left: "White Horse Scotch Whisky" plaster compound figure, 23cm (9″) high, AUS $125-150; US $80-95; £50-60.

Far left: "White Horse Scotch Whisky" plaster compound figure, 13cm (5″) high, AUS $150-180; US $100-120; £60-70.

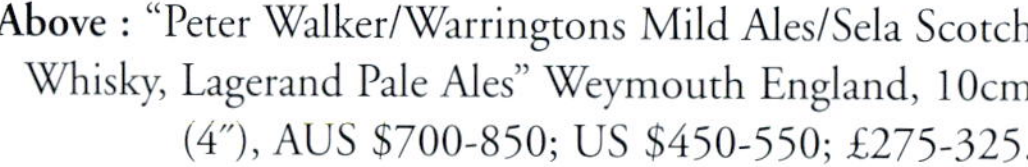

Above : "Peter Walker/Warringtons Mild Ales/Sela Scotch Whisky, Lagerand Pale Ales" Weymouth England, 10cm (4″), AUS $700-850; US $450-550; £275-325.

Above right: "Williams's Aberdeen Whisky" glass decanter, white enamel paint, 26cm (10¼″) high, AUS $250-300; US $150-180; £100-120.

Right: "Whyte & Mackay Scotch Whisky" Wade, 16.5cm (6½″), AUS $65-75; US $40-50; £25-30.

Lower right: "Whyte & Mackay Scotch Whisky" Wade, 14cm (5½″), AUS $65-75; US $40-50; £25-30.

Below left: "White Queen Whisky" Derbyshire, 16.5cm (6½″), AUS $85-100; US $55-70; £35-40.

Below centre: "Western Isles Highland Whisky" Staffordshire, 15cm (6″), AUS $85-100; US $55-70; £35-40.

Below right: "Wilson's Matured Blend Whisky" no base mark, 16.5cm (6½″), AUS $130-160; US $85-100; £50-60.

Above: "White Heather Whisky" no base mark, 15cm (6″), AUS $400-500; US $250-310; £160-185.

Right: "White Heather Deluxe Blended Scotch Whisky" handpainted porcelain decanter, distiller's name on base, 38cm (15″) high, AUS $125-150; US $80-95; £50-60.

"White Heather Scotch Whisky" Euroceramics, 21cm (8¼″) high, twice the capacity of normal jugs, AUS $170-200; US $110-30; £65-75.

"White Heather Scotch Whisky" Euroceramics, standard size, 15cm (6″) high, AUS $85-100; US $55-65; £35-40.

Above: "Johnny Wright's Blended Scotch Whisky" Wade Regicor, 10cm (4″), AUS $300-350; US $180-210; £120-140.

Right: "Wm. Williams & Sons Highland Whisky" glass back bar dispenser, etched print painted in gold, 72cm (28½″) high, AUS $2500-3000; US $1600-1900; £1000-1250.

Below left: "Wright & Greig's Premier Old Scotch Whisky" Wm. Brownlie, 14cm (5½″), AUS $700-800; US $450-525; £275-325.

Below right: "Ye Monks Curious Old Whisky" Wade PDM, 11cm (4½″), AUS $300-350; US $190-220; £120-140.

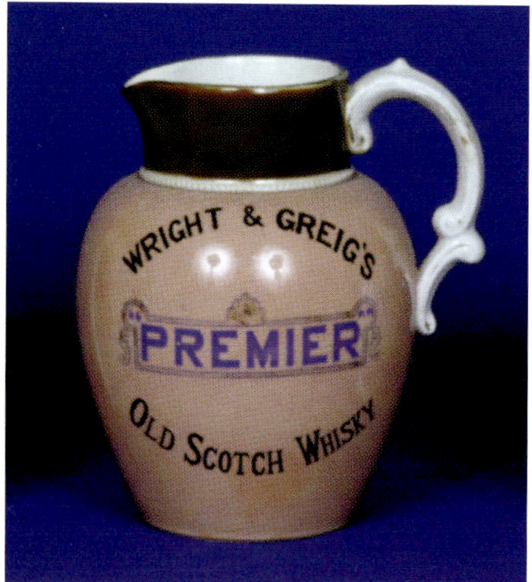

Above left: "Worthington In Bottle" Fieldings, England, 16.5cm (6½"), AUS $200-250; US $130-160; £80-100.

Above right: "Worthington In Bottle" Mintons, 11cm (4¼"), AUS $300-350; US $180-210; £120-140.

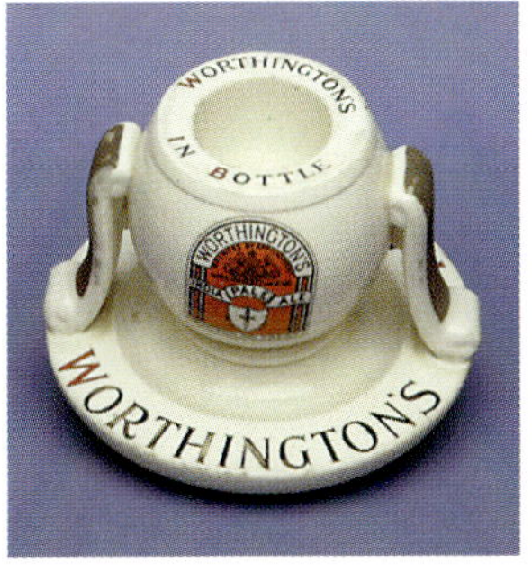

Right: "Worthington's Pale Ale" matchstriker, Royal Doulton, 15cm (6") dia, AUS $350-400; US $225-255; £140-160.

Below left: "Worthington's India Pale Ale" W.T. Copeland, produced in 1902 to celebrate the Coronation of King Edward VII, blue & black print, 17cm (6¾"), AUS $1000-1250; US $650-750; £400-500. **Below centre:** "Worthington's India Pale Ale" brewer's name on base, 15.5cm (6"), AUS $500-600; US $325-375; £200-250. **Below right:** "Worthington's India Pale Ale" magnificent jug, produced to celebrate the Coronation of King Edward VII in 1902, W.T. Copeland & Son, 17cm (6¾"), AUS $2000-2500; US $1250-1500; £750-850.

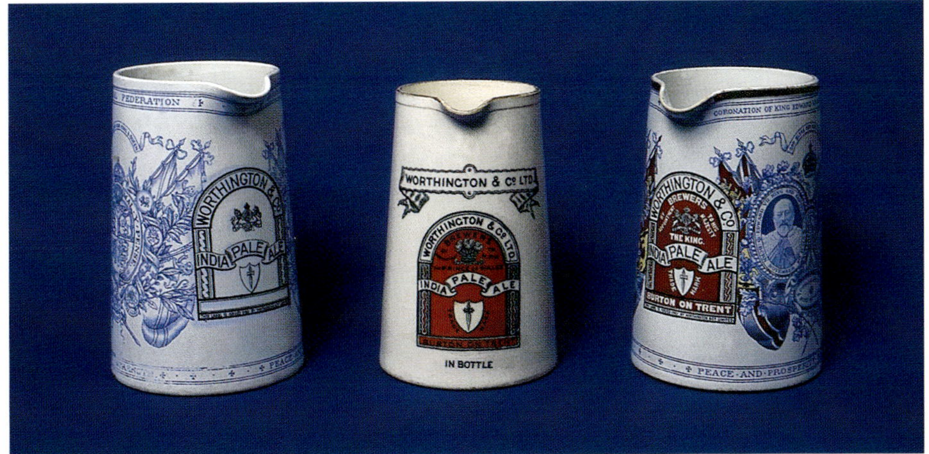

Left: "Whitbread's Pale Ale - Good for him & Good for You since Seventeen Hundred & Forty Two" cast metal figure, 39cm (15½″) high, AUS $1000-1250; US $650-800; £400-500.

Above: "Whitbread's Bottled Beers" matchstriker, 10cm (4″) high, AUS $500-600; US $300-360; £200-250.

"Worthington" Ales match-striker, Fieldings, 9cm (3½″) high, AUS $325-375; US $210-240; £125-145.

"Worthington" Ales, Mintons, England, 15 x 12cm (6 x 4¾″), AUS $250-300; US $150-180; £100-120.

"Ask for Worthington In Bottle" Raphael Tuck & Sons London, 6 x 10cm (2½ x 4″), AUS $325-375; US $210-240; £125-145.

"Younger's Tartan Beer" rubber compound figure, 23cm (9″) high. This figure is missing a tankard of beer and a walking cane, AUS $400-475; US $250-300; £160-185.

"Wills & Sons' Fine Shag" tobacco ceramic figure, 37cm (14½″) high, AUS $1000-1250; US $650-800; £400-500.

"Williams & Humberts Walnut Brown Sherry" rubber compound figure, 27cm (10½″) high, AUS $800-1000; US $500-625; £325-400.

"W.D. & H.O. Wills Westward Ho!" tobacco match-holder, no base mark, 9cm (3½″) dia, AUS $225-275; US $150-180; £90-110.

BACK COVER: Top, left to right: "Captain Morgan Rum" rubber compound figure, 32cm (12½") high, AUS $600-750; US $400-500; £240-280. "James Buchanan & Coy. Ltd," framed tin advertisement 38 x 33cm (15 X 13"), AUS $1000-1250; US $650-800; £400-500. "Greenlees Brothers Ancient Old Parr Antique Scotch Whisky" porcelain figure, 40cm (15¾") high, AUS $4000-4500; US $2600-3000; £1600-1800.

Centre, left to right: "King George IV Old Scotch Whisky" no base stamp, 9cm (3½"), AUS $350-400; US $225-255; £140-160. "Huntsman Ales" James Green & Nephew, 10cm (4"), AUS $600-700; US $375-450; £240-280. "Buchanan's Black & White" 15cm (6"), AUS $3500-4000; US $2250-2550, £1400-1600. "Grant's Stand Fast Whisky" HCW, 8cm (3¼"), AUS $400-500; US $250-300; £160-200. "Bulloch Lade Scotch Whisky" Shelley, 10.5cm (4¼"), AUS $450-500; US $275-325; £175-200. "Old Charlie Fine Jamaica Rum" Fieldings, 10cm (4"), AUS $450-525; US $300-330; £175-200.

Front, left to right: "John Haig's Whisky" ashtray, Fieldings, 14 x 12cm (5½ x 4¾"), AUS $300-350; US $200-230; £120-140. "D.C.L. Scotch Whisky" ashtray, Doulton Burslem, 10 x 7cm (4 x 2¾"), AUS $325-400; US $225-275; £125-150. "Watson's Blue Band" match-holder/ashtray, Shelley, 14.5 x 10cm (5½ x 4"), AUS $500-600; US $300-350; £200-230.

Alphabetical Index

Alphabetical Index

Alphabetical Index

Abbreviation Descriptions

ab	Ashbowl	ca	Calendar	m	Measure
ad	Advertisement	cb	Counter Bell	me	Menu holder
at	Ashtray	cd	Cigarette Dispenser	mh	Match-holder
bb	Biscuit Barrel	ct	Change Tray	ms	Match-striker
bd	Back Bar Dispenser	dc	Display Card	pc	Postcard
bf	Bar Figure	de	Decanter	pl	Plate
bk	Book	ds	Dice Shaker	plc	Playing Cards
bo	Bottle	gf	Glass Flask	tj	Toby Jug
bt	Bar Tray	ib	Ice Bucket	ts	Tin Sign
c	Clock	j	Jug	wc	Water Carafe

Alphabetical Index

Alphabetical Index

Abbreviation Descriptions

ab Ashbowl
ad Advertisement
at Ashtray
bb Biscuit Barrel
bd Back Bar Dispenser
bf Bar Figure
bk Book
bo Bottle
bt Bar Tray
c Clock
ca Calendar
cb Counter Bell
cd Cigarette Dispenser
ct Change Tray
dc Display Card
de Decanter
ds Dice Shaker
gf Glass Flask
ib Ice Bucket
j Jug
m Measure
me Menu holder
mh Match-holder
ms Match-striker
pc Postcard
pl Plate
plc Playing Cards
tj Toby Jug
ts Tin Sign
wc Water Carafe

Revised Valuations for 1991 Edition

International Currency Conversion Chart

AUS	USA	UK	AUS	USA	UK	AUS	USA	UK
$25	$16	£10	$425	$275	£170	$825	$535	£330
$50	$33	£20	$450	$290	£180	$850	$550	£340
$75	$49	£30	$475	$310	£190	$875	$565	£350
$100	$65	£40	$500	$325	£200	$900	$585	£360
$125	$80	£50	$525	$340	£210	$925	$600	£370
$150	$95	£60	$550	$355	£220	$950	$615	£380
$175	$110	£70	$575	$370	£230	$975	$630	£390
$200	$130	£80	$600	$390	£240	$1000	$650	£400
$225	$145	£90	$625	$405	£250	$1200	$780	£480
$250	$160	£100	$650	$420	£260	$1400	$910	£560
$275	$175	£110	$675	$435	£270	$1600	$1040	£640
$300	$195	£120	$700	$455	£280	$1800	$1170	£720
$325	$210	£130	$725	$470	£290	$2000	$1300	£800
$350	$230	£140	$750	$485	£300	$3000	$1950	£1200
$375	$245	£150	$775	$500	£310	$4000	$2600	£1600
$400	$260	£160	$800	$520	£320	$5000	$3250	£2000

Page 17

Bottom left: "Gaelic Old Smuggler" $1500-2000.

Bottom centre: "Usher's Pale Ales" $1200-1500.

Bottom right: "Sandy Macdonald" $1500-2000.

Page 19

Centre two: "Buchanan's Special Red Seal" $2300-2700.

Page 25

Centre right: "Ainslie's" $3000-3500.

Bottom left: "Ainslie's" $550-650.

Bottom centre: "Arrowsmith's" $500-600.

Bottom right: "Ainslie's" $600-750.

Page 26

Top left: "Ainslie's" $200-250.

Top centre: "Army & Navy" $550-650.

Top right: "Ambassador" $175-225.

Centre left: "Abbot's Choice" $200-250.

Centre: "The Antiquary" $65-75.

Centre right: "Aberlour Glenlivet" $80-100.

Centre left (below): "Abbot's Choice" $150-175.

Bottom left: "Ambassador" $175-200.

Bottom centre: "Ambassador" $175-200.

Bottom right: "Ambassador" $150-175.

Page 27
Top left: "John Barr" $100-120.
Top centre: "Ballantine's" $70-90.
Top right: "Bartel's Scotch" $140-165.
Centre left: "Ballantine's" $90-120.
Centre (above): "Ballantine's" (blue) $70-90.
Centre (below): "Ballantine's" (pale yellow) $90-120.
Centre right: "Ballantine's" $350-450.
Bottom left: "Ballantine's" $120-150.
Bottom centre: "Ballantrae" $500-600.
Bottom right: "Ballantine's" $50-65.

Page 28
Top left: "John Begg" $150-200.
Top centre: "John Begg" $300-350.
Top right: "John Begg" $250-300.
Centre: "John Begg" $80-100.
Bottom left: "John Begg" $550-700.
Bottom centre: "Jamie Stuart" $800-1000.
Bottom right: "John Begg" $850-1000.

Page 29
Top left: "Bell's" $65-85.
Top centre: "Bell's" $250-300.
Top right: "Bell's" $55-65.
Centre: "Arthur Bell" $250-300.
Bottom left: "Benlovit" $450-500.
Bottom centre: "Arthur Bell" $65-75.
Bottom right: "Bell's" $70-85.

Page 31
Top left: "Buchanan's" $3000-3500.
Top centre: "Buchanan's" $1400-1800.
Top right: "Buchanan's" $3000-3500.

Page 32
Top left: "Buchanan's" $4500-5500.
Bottom left: "Buchanan's" $3500-4000.
Bottom right: "Buchanan's" $3500-4000.

Page 33
Top left: "Buchanan's" $3500-4000.
Top centre: "Buchanan's" $200-250.
Top right: "Buchanan's" $3500-4000.
Centre left: "Buchanan" $100-125.
Centre: "Buchanan" $140-165.
Centre right: "Black & White" $175-225.
Bottom left: "Black & White" $600-700.
Bottom right: "Buchanan's" $1500-2000.

Page 34
Top left: "Black & White" $250-300.
Top centre: "Black & White" $50-60.
Top right: "Black & White" $500-600.
Centre left: "Black & White" $225-275.
Centre right: "Black & White" $225-275.
Bottom left: "Black & White" $650-750.
Bottom right: "Buchanan's" $3000-3500.

Page 35
Top left: "Black & White" $50-60.
Top centre: "Black & White" $100-130.
Top right: "Black & White" $55-65.
Centre left: "Black & White" $1000-1250.
Centre right: "Buchanan's" $600-700.
Bottom left: "Buchanan's $400-500.
Bottom right: "Buchanan's" $650-750.

Page 36
Bottom left, centre & right: "Buchanan's" $1400-1800 each.

Page 38
Top left: "Bulloch Lade" $450-500.
Top centre: "Bulloch Lade" $300-350.

Top right: "Bulloch Lade" $450-500.

Centre right: "B.L." $150-200.

Bottom left: "Bulloch Lade" $350-400.

Bottom centre: "Bulloch Lade" $550-700.

Bottom right: "Bulloch Lade" $400-450.

Page 39

Top left: "Bowmore" $90-120.

Top centre: "Black Bottle" $70-90.

Top right: "Big T" $90-120.

Centre left: "Black Douglas" $70-80.

Centre: "Black Bottle" $75-90.

Centre right: "Black Douglas" $90-120.

Bottom left: "Burke's" $700-850.

Bottom centre: "Black Bottle" $90-120.

Bottom right: "Black & White & Brilliant" $140-180.

Page 40

Top left: "Beneagles" $150-200.

Top centre: "Black & White/Cossack" $90-120.

Top right: "Bruichladdich" $75-85.

Centre left: "Black Jack" $80-100.

Centre: "Bonnie Charlie" $120-150.

Centre right: "Big Ben" $100-120.

Bottom left: "Buchanan & Currie" $550-700.

Bottom right: "Robbie Burns" $1500-2000.

Page 41

Top left: "Black Bull" $550-700.

Top centre: "Black & White" $400r-450.

Top right: "Old Bushmills" $500-600.

Centre right: "Brown & Co." $900-1200.

Bottom left: "James Buchanan" $2000-2500.

Bottom centre: "Robbie Burns" $1200-1500.

Bottom right: "Baxter's" $750-900

Page 42

Top left: "Cluny" $60-75.

Top centre: "Claymore" $450-550.

Top right: "Clan Campbell" $75-90.

Centre left: "Craigmhor" $125-150.

Centre (above): "Chivas Regal" $175-225.

Centre (below): "Catto's" $500-600.

Centre right: "Cromarty" $100-130.

Bottom left: "Cluny" $100-130.

Bottom centre: "Cluny" $220-250.

Bottom right: "Cluny" $90-120.

Page 43

Top left: "Chivas Regal" $80-100.

Top centre: "Canadian Club" $150-175.

Top right: "Clan Campbell" $25-35.

Centre left: "Claymore" $900-1200.

Centre: "Claymore" $550-700.

Centre right: "Claymore" $600-750.

Bottom left: "Paul Dainty" $1200-1500.

Bottom centre: "Claymore" $1200-1500.

Bottom right: "Bailie Nicol Jarvie" $900-1200.

Page 45

Top left: "Crawford's" $80-100.

Top centre: "Daniel Crawford's" $250-300.

Top right: "Daniel Crawford's" $220-250.

Centre left (top): "Daniel Crawford's" $250-300.

Centre (top): "Crawford's" $120-150.

Centre right (top): "Crawford's" $100-130.

Centre left (below): "Chivas Regal" $110-140.

Centre below: "Catto's" $90-120.

Centre right (below): "Daniel Crawford's" $250-300.

Bottom left: "Chesters" $550-700.

Bottom centre: "Daniel Crawford's" $250-300.

Bottom right: "Cowan's" $350-400.

Page 46

Top left: "Crawford's" $350-400.

Top centre: "Cutty Sark" $250-300

Top right: "Cutty Sark" $200-250.

Centre left: "Claymore" $250-300.

Centre: "Cutty Sark" $90-120.

Centre right: "Cutty Sark" $200-250.

Bottom left: "Cutty Sark" $200-250.

Bottom centre: "Cutty Sark" $75-90.

Bottom right: "Cutty Sark" $200-250.

Page 47

Top left: "Peter Dawson's" $650-750.

Top centre: "Doctors' Special" $170-200.

Top right: "Peter Dawson's" $650-750.

Centre left: "Peter Dawson" $250-300.

Centre: "Dawson's" $450-500.

Centre right: "Dickens" $350-400.

Bottom: Tray $90-120.

Page 48

Top left: "Peter Dawson" $350-400.

Top centre: "Peter Dawson" $450-500.

Top right: "Peter Dawson" $200-250.

Centre left: "Peter Dawson" $60-75.

Centre: "Peter Dawson's" $1000-1250.

Centre right: "Peter Dawson" $80-100.

Bottom left: "Peter Dawson" $200-250.

Bottom centre: "Peter Dawson" $350-400.

Bottom right: "Peter Dawson" $200-250.

Page 49

Top left: "Duff's" $350-400.

Top centre & right: "Dunville's" $450-550.

Centre left (top): "Dunville's" $250-300.

Centre left (bottom): "Dunville's" $200-250.

Centre: "Mitchells & Butlers" $450-500.

Centre right: "Dimple" $70-85.

Bottom left: "Dandie Dinmont" $250-300.

Bottom right: "Dandie Dinmont" $850-1050.

Page 51

Top left: "D.C.L." $300-350.

Top centre: "D.C.L." $350-400.

Top right: "D.C.L." $350-400.

Centre left: "D.C.L." $700-800.

Centre: "Combe's" $600-700.

Centre right: "D.W.D." $450-500.

Bottom left: "Dandie Dinmont" $1200-1500.

Bottom centre: "Dandie Dinmont" $1500-2000.

Bottom right: "D.C.L." $650-750.

Page 52

Bottom left: "John Dewar & Sons"

$450-550.

Page 53

Bottom left: "Dewar's White Label"

$400-450.

Bottom right: "Dewar's Imperial" $700-800.

Page 54

Top left: "Dewar's" $100-130.

Top centre: "Dewar's" $70-90.

Top right: "Dewar's" $175-225.

Centre left: “Dewar’s” (white) $120-150.
Centre right: “Dewar’s” (yellow) $80-100.
Bottom left: “Dewar’s Ancestor” $150-200.
Bottom centre: “Dewar’s” $120-150.
Bottom right: “Dewar’s” $80-100.

Page 55
Top left: “Dewar’s” $800-1000.
Top centre: “Dewar’s” $1000-1250.
Top right: “Blundell’s” $1000-1200.
Bottom right: “Dewar’s” $400-500.

Page 58
Top left: “Dewar’s” $250-300.
Top centre: “Dewar’s” $100-120.
Top right: “Dewar’s” $300-350.
Centre left (top): “Dewar’s” $250-300.
Centre left (bottom): “Dewar’s” $350-400.
Centre: “Dewar’s” $150-200.
Centre right (top): “Dewar’s” $250-300.
Centre right (bottom): Dewar’s” $450-500.
Bottom left: “Dewar’s” $220-250.
Bottom centre: “Dewar’s” $90-110.
Bottom right: “Dewar’s” $125-150.

Page 59
Top left: “Dewar’s” $150-200.
Top centre: “Dewar’s” $150-200.
Top right: “Dewar’s” $150-200.
Bottom left: “Encore” $800-1000.
Bottom centre: “Duniva” $900-1200.
Bottom right: “Duniva” $1200-1500.

Page 60
Top left: “Famous Grouse” $250-300.
Top centre: “Four Seasons” $100-130.
Top right: “Famous Grouse” $100-130.
Centre left: “Four Seasons” $90-120.
Centre: “Famous Grouse” $60-80.
Centre right: “Findlaters” $60-75.
Bottom left: “Famous Grouse” $120-150.
Bottom right: “Four Seasons” $65-75.

Page 61
Top left: “Grant’s Standfast” $400-500.
Centre left: “Grant’s” $65-75.
Centre right: “Grant’s” $1500-2000.
Bottom left: “Grant’s” $400-450.
Bottom centre: “Grant’s” $600-700.
Bottom right: “Grant’s” $600-700.

Page 62
Top left: “Grant’s” $175-225.
Top centre: “Grant’s” $175-200.
Top right: “Grant’s” $100-130.
Centre left: “Grant’s $150-200.
Centre: “Grant’s” $350-400.
Centre right: “J. & G. Grant” $120-150.
Bottom right: “Grant’s” $65-75.

Page 63
Top left: “G.O.H.” $300- 350.
Top centre left: “Old Mull” $150-175.
Top centre right: “Haig” $600-800.
Top right: “G.O.H.” $300-350
Centre left: “Gillon’s” $700-800.
Centre: “Haig & Haig” $800-900.
Centre right: “Gillon’s” $600-700.
Bottom left: “King’s Cross” $1000-1200.
Bottom centre: “Usher’s” $800-1000.
Bottom right: “Loch Katrine” $1200-1500.

Page 64
Top left: “Greer’s” $300-350.
Top centre: “Greer’s” $350-400.
Top right: “Greer’s” $400-450.

Centre left: "Glen Garry" $120-150.

Centre: "Glen Elgin" $150- 200.

Centre right: "Glen Garry" $120-150.

Bottom left: "Glengoyne" $80-100.

Bottom centre: "Glen Garioch" $150-200.

Bottom right: "Gold Thimble" $65-75.

Page 65

Top left: "William Whiteley" $800-1000.

Top centre: "M.B. Foster" $1500-2000.

Top right: "Slater, Rodger & Co." $900-1200.

Bottom: "Gilbey's" (tray) $500-650.

Page 66

Top left: "Glen Eagle" $90-120.

Top centre: "Glenfiddich" $90-120.

Top right: "Grand Macnish" $140-170.

Centre left (top): "Glenmorangie" $75-90.

Centre left (bottom): "Gilbey's" $220-250.

Centre: "Grand Old Highland" $90-110.

Centre right: "Glenfarclas" $110-130.

Bottom left: "Glenfarclas" $75-90.

Bottom centre: "Glengoyne" $250-300.

Bottom right: "Glen Adam" $75-90.

Page 67

Top left: "Haig" $70-80.

Top centre: "John Haig's" $300-350.

Top right: "John Haig" $300-350.

Bottom left: "Haig & Haig" $400-450.

Bottom centre: "Haig & Haig" $800-1000.

Bottom right: "Haigs" $400-450.

Page 68

Top left: "Haig" $150-200.

Top centre: "Haig" $65-80.

Top right: "Haig" $150-200.

Centre left (top): "Haig's" $200-250.

Centre left (bottom): "Haig & Haig" $300-350.

Centre: "Haig" $150-200.

Centre right: "Haig" $70-80.

Bottom left: "John Haig's" $300-350.

Bottom right: "John Haig's" $550-650.

Page 70

Top left: "Hopkins" $400- 450.

Top centre: "Huntly Blend" $600-700.

Top right: "Hedges & Butler" $90-120.

Centre left: "Highland Queen" $100-125.

Centre: "Harvey's" $350-400.

Centre right (top): "Rare Old Highland Nectar" $80-100.

Centre right (bottom): "Heather Dew" $350-400.

Bottom left: "Hill, Thomson & Co." $350-400.

Bottom right: "Heatherdale" $350-400.

Page 71

Top left: "John Haig's" $800-1000.

Top centre: "Haig's Glenleven"

$1200-1500.

Top right: "John Haig's" $550-650.

Centre left: "John Haig" $800-1000.

Centre: "Georges' Beers" $750-850.

Centre right: "Hansons Bonnie Dundee" $800-1000.

Bottom left: "John Haig" $250-300.

Bottom centre: "Vat 69" $700-850.

Bottom right: "Strong's" $450-550.

Page 72

Top left: "J & B" $60-70

Top centre: "Highland Fusilier" $120-150.

Top right: "House of Lords" $175-225.

Centre left: “Isle of Jura” $80-100.

Centre: “Highland Queen” $80-95.

Centre right: “Inver House” $75-90.

Bottom left: “Jameson” $100-120.

Bottom centre: “Inverness Cream” $75-85.

Bottom right: “J & B” $90-120.

Page 73

Top left: “Huntsman Ales” $600-700.

Top centre: “Meynell Hunt” $750-900.

Top right: “Huntsman Brand” $500-550.

Centre left: “Highland Queen” $500-600.

Centre: “Heather Dew” $500-600.

Centre right: “Highland Queen” $600-700.

Bottom left: “Killingley’s” $450-550.

Bottom centre: “King George IV” $800-1000.

Bottom right: “Lowrie’s” $500-550.

Page 74

Top left: “King’s Ransom” $175-225.

Top centre: “King George IV” $90-120.

Top right: “King George IV” $750-850.

Centre left: “King George IV” $60-70.

Centre: “King George IV” $650-750.

Centre right: “King of Scots” $125-150.

Bottom left: “King George IV” $900-1200.

Bottom right: “King’s Ransom” $400-500.

Page 75

Left: “D.C.L.” $500-600.

Right: “King George IV” $500-600.

Page 76

Top left: “King George IV” $90-120.

Top centre: “King George IV” $350-400.

Top right: “King George IV” $120-150.

Centre left: “King George IV” $800-1000.

Centre: “King George IV” (ashtray) $350-400.

Centre right: “King George IV” $700-800.

Bottom left: “King George IV” $500-600.

Bottom centre: “King George IV” $450-550

Bottom right: “King George IV” $500-600.

Page 78

Top left: “Lauder’s” $120-150.

Top centre: “Larvar Jarvar” $400-450.

Top right: “Lauder’s” $120-150.

Centre left: “Lang’s” $250-300.

Centre: “Lang’s” $80-100.

Centre right: “Laphroaig” $120-150.

Bottom left: “Lang’s” $80-100.

Bottom centre: Lang’s” $80-100.

Bottom right: “Lang’s” $75-90.

Page 79

Top left: “Laphroaig” $90- 110.

Top centre: “William Lawson’s” $75-90.

Top right: “Lauder’s” $150-175.

Centre left: “Lowrie’s” $100-130.

Centre: “Lowrie” $350-400.

Centre right: “King’s Council” $900-1200.

Bottom left: “King’s Liqueur” $900-1200.

Bottom centre: “King’s Liqueur” $600-700.

Bottom right: “Muscroft’s” $1200-1500.

Page 80

Centre left: “Long John” $200-250.

Bottom left: “Long John” $75-85.

Bottom centre: “Long John” $65-75.

Bottom right: “Long John” $110-130.

Page 81

Top left: “Mackinlay’s” $65-75.

Top centre: "Real Mackenzie" $110-130.

Top right: "Original Mackinlay" $75-90.

Centre left: "Mackinlay's" $65-75.

Centre (top): "Great Macaulay" $80-100.

Centre (bottom): "Real Mackenzie" $300-350.

Centre right: "Martin's V.V.O." $90-110.

Bottom left: "Macallan" $80-100.

Bottom centre: " Melrose Drover" $350-400.

Bottom right: "Mackinlay's" $60-75.

Page 82

Top left: "Macnish" $110-130.

Top centre: "Duncan MacGregor" $120-150.

Top right: "Macnish" $110-130.

Second row, left: "McNish" $400-450.

Second row, centre: "McNish" $300-350.

Second row, right: "McNish's" $400-450.

Third row, left: "Macleay Duff" $90-110.

Third row, centre: "Macleay Duff" $65-75.

Third row, right: "Macleay Duff" $120-150.

Bottom left: "Macleay Duff" $150-175.

Bottom centre: "Macleay Duff" $300-350.

Bottom right: "Macleay Duff" $80-100.

Page 83

Bottom left: "McCallum" $250-300.

Bottom centre: "McCallum" $200-250.

Bottom right: "McCallum" $200-250.

Page 84

Top left: "McEwan's" $500-600.

Top centre: "Mitchell's" $450-500.

Top right: "McCallum's" $200-250.

Centre left (top): "McCallum's" $65-85.

Centre left (bottom): "Milne's" $200-250.

Centre: "McCallum's" $40-45.

Centre right: "C & J McDonald" $90-110.

Bottom left: "McCallum's" $150-200.

Bottom centre: "Munro's" $200-250.

Bottom right: "Macallan" $75-85.

Page 85

Top left: "McCallum" $70-80.

Top centre: "McCallum" $70-80.

Top right: "McCallum" $70-80.

Centre left: "McCallum" $650-750.

Centre right: "McCallum's" $650-750.

Bottom left: "McCallum's" $500-600.

Bottom centre: "McCallum's" $750-850

Bottom right: "McCallum's" $750-850.

Page 86

Top left: "McNish's" $2500-3000.

Top right: "McNish's" $750-900.

Bottom left: "John Murray" $800-900.

Bottom centre: "Poole & Anderson's" $750-850.

Bottom right: "James Munro" $750-850.

Page 87

Top left: "Old Parr" $90-110.

Top centre: "Old Moses" $200-250.

Top right: "Mac's Own" $700-850.

Centre left: "Offiler's" $1000-1200.

Centre: "Roderick Dhu" $700-850.

Centre right: "Old Style" $450-500.

Bottom left: "Pattisons" $800-1000.

Bottom centre: "Old Mull" $500-600.

Bottom right: "Old Mull" $400-450.

Page 88

Top left: "Paddy" $80-100.

Top centre: "Old Store" $400-450.

Top right: "Power's" $110-130.

Centre left: "Paddy" $125-150.

Centre: "Old Bushmills" $170-200.

Centre right: "Paddy" $120-150.

Bottom left: "Old Trad" $120-150.

Bottom centre: "House of Peers" $120-150.

Bottom right (top): "Old Rarity" $140-170.

Bottom right: "Old Mull" $150-175.

Page 90

Left: "Pick Kwik" $200-250.

Right: "Dewar's" $200-250.

Page 91

Top left: "Mitchells & Butler" $500-600.

Top centre left: "Eadie's Gleneagles" $700-900.

Top centre right: "Mitchells & Butlers" $500-600.

Top right: "Mitchells & Butler" $500-600.

Centre left: "Macleay Duff" $500-600.

Centre: "Isleworth Fine Ales" $800-1000.

Right: "Redlan Whisky" $450-500.

Bottom left: "O.V.H." $450-500.

Bottom centre: "Quinol" $400-450.

Bottom right: "O.V.H." $450-500.

Page 92

Top left: "Old Smuggler" $120-150.

Top centre: "Old Smuggler" $80-100.

Top right: "Old Smuggler" $200-250.

Centre left: "Gaelic Old Smuggler" $1500-2000.

Centre: "Passport" $90-120.

Centre right: "Old Smuggler" $140-180.

Bottom left: "Passport" $70-85.

Bottom centre: "Old Smuggler" $700-850.

Bottom right: "Passport" $100-120.

Page 93

Top right: "Old Smugger" (figure) $400-500.

Bottom left: "Old Smuggler" $300-350.

Bottom right: "Old Smuggler" (Royal Norfolk) $450-500. (Piola) $150-200.

Page 94

Top left: "Queen Anne" $100-120.

Top centre: "Queen Anne" $90-100.

Top right: "Queen Anne" $120-150.

Centre: "Queen Anne" $400-450.

Bottom left: "Queen Anne" $110-130.

Bottom centre: "Queen Anne" $175-225.

Bottom right: "Queen Anne" $120-150.

Page 95

Top left: "Queen Margaret" $100-120.

Top centre: "John Power's" $110-130.

Top right: "Red Hackle" $90-110.

Centre left: "Queen Anne" $175-200.

Centre: "Red Tape" $800-1000.

Centre right: "Queen Anne" $150-175.

Bottom left: "Queen o' the Spey" $70-85.

Bottom centre: "Red Hackle" $65-80.

Bottom right: "Royal Culross" $90-110.

Page 97

Top left: "Sandy MacDonald" $220-250.

Top centre: "Robertson's" $250-300.

Top right: "Sandeman" $300-350.

Centre left: "Scots Grey" $80-95.

Centre: "Scottish Cream" $80-100.

Centre right: "Saltyre" $75-85.

Bottom left: "Rob Roy" $550-650.

Bottom centre: "Sanderson's" $450-500.

Bottom right: "Scottish Cream" $250-300.

Page 98

Top left: "Seagram's" $125-150.

Top centre: "Seagram's" $65-75.

Top right: "100 Pipers" $90-110.

Bottom left: "Seagrams" $110-130.

Bottom centre: "Hundred Pipers" $170-200.

Bottom right: "Seagram's" $80-100.

Page 99

Top left: "Jamie Stuart" $150-175.

Top centre: "Something Special" $75-90.

Top right: "Strong's" $400-450.

Centre left: "Stewart's" $80-90.

Centre: "Piper" $90-110.

Centre right: "Suntory" $90-110.

Bottom left: "100 Pipers" $110-130.

Bottom centre: "Seagram's" $100-120.

Bottom right: "Springbank" $110-130.

Page 100

Top left: "Stewart's" $250-300.

Top right: "Stronachie Distillery" $1500-2000.

Centre left: "House of Stuart" $170-200.

Bottom left: "Sir Edward Lees" $900-1200.

Bottom right: "Roderick Dhu" $450-500.

Page 101

Top left: "Stewart's" $150-175.

Top centre: "Sykes'" $200-250.

Top right: "Jamie Stuart" $200-225.

Centre left: "J. & G. Stewart" $750-850.

Centre: "Simpson's" $700-800.

Centre right: "J. & G. Stewart's" $600-700.

Bottom left: "Stenhouse" $1000-1250.

Bottom centre: "Stenhouse" $1500-2000.

Bottom right: "Alexander & MacDonald" $600-700.

Page 102

Bottom left: "Teacher's" $250-300.

Bottom centre: "Teacher's" $250-300.

Bottom right: "Teacher's" $600-700.

Page 103

Top left: "Teacher's" $110-130.

Top centre: "Teacher's" $650-750.

Top right: "Teacher's" $200-230.

Centre left: "Teacher's" $75-90.

Centre (top): Teacher's" $250-300.

Centre (bottom): "Teacher's") $150-175.

Centre right: "Teacher's" $55-65.

Bottom left: "Teacher's" $55-65.

Bottom centre: "Teacher's" $220-250.

Bottom right: "Teacher's" $250-300.

Page 104

Centre left: "Thorne's" $850-1000.

Centre right: "Thorne's" $750-850.

Bottom left: "Thorne's" $750-850.

Bottom centre: "Teacher's" $800-1000.

Bottom right: "Thorne's" $900-1200.

Page 105

Top left: "Tullibardine" $70-85.

Top right: "Thorne's" $1000-1250.

Centre left: "Taplow's" $150-175.

Bottom left: "Talisker" $300-325.

Bottom right: "Thorne's" $1000-1250.

Page 106

Top left: "Usher's" $450-500.

Top right: "Usher's" $450-500.

Bottom left: "Usher's" $700-850.

Bottom centre: "Usher's" $600-700.

Bottom right: "Uam-Var" $900-1200.

Page 107

Top left: "Vat 69" $175-200.

Top centre: "Vat 69" $60-70.

Top right: "Usher's" $110-130.

Centre left: "Vat 69" $200-225.

Centre: "Vat 69" $40-50.

Centre right: "Vat 69" $200-225.

Third row, left: "William's" $200-250.

Third row, right: "Vat 69" $80-90.

Bottom left: "Victoria Club" $90-110.

Bottom centre: "William's" $450-500.

Bottom right: "White Heather" $75-90.

Page 108

Bottom left: "Johnnie Walker" $2000-2500.

Bottom centre: "Johnnie Walker" $900-1200.

Bottom right: "Johnnie Walker" $2500-3000.

Page 109

Framed advert: "Johnnie Walker" $1200-1500.

Page 110

Top left: "Johnnie Walker" $75-90.

Top centre: "Johnnie Walker" $75-90.

Top right: "Johnnie Walker" $300-350.

Centre left: "Johnnie Walker" $70-85.

Centre: "Johnnie Walker" $90-110.

Centre right: "Johnnie Walker" $90-110.

Bottom left: "Johnnie Walker" $350-400.

Bottom centre: "Johnnie Walker" $220-250.

Bottom right: "Johnnie Walker" $175-200.

Page 111

Top right: "Johnnie Walker" $800-1000.

Bottom left: "Johnnie Walker" toby jug $2500-3000. (1920's era)

Bottom right: "Johnnie Walker" figure $500-700 (depending on condition).

Page 112

Top left: "Johnnie Walker" $300-350.

Top centre: "Johnnie Walker" $350-400.

Top right: "Johnnie Walker" $400-450.

Centre left: "Johnnie Walker" $150-200.

Centre: "Johnnie Walker" $90-110.

Centre right: "Johnnie Walker" $110-130.

Bottom left: "Johnnie Walker" $80-90.

Bottom centre: "Johnnie Walker" $100-130.

Bottom right: "Johnnie Walker" $350-450.

Page 113

Top left: "Johnnie Walker" $110-130.

Top centre: "Walker's" $250-300.

Top right: "Johnnie Walker" $150-175.

Centre left: "Whyte & Mackay's" $55-65.

Centre: "Whyte & Mackay" $55-65.

Centre right: "Whyte & Mackay" $60-75.

Bottom left: "Whyte & Mackay" $90-110.

Bottom centre: "Johnnie Walker" $90-110.

Bottom right: "Johnnie Walker" $110-130.

Page 114

Bottom right: "White Horse" $80-90.

Page 115

Top left: "White Horse" $700-800.

Top centre: "Greer's" $600-700.

Top right: "White Horse" $1000-1200.

Centre left: "Mackie's White Horse" $1200-1500.

Centre: "Greyhound" $1000-1250.

Centre right: "Mackie's Greyhound" $1200-1500.

Bottom left: "White Horse" $1000-1250.

Bottom centre: "White Horse" (ashtray) $300-350.

Bottom right: "White Horse" $2000-2500.

Page 116

Top left: "White Horse" $50-60.

Top centre: "White Horse" $150-175.

Top right: "Watson's" $200-225.

Centre left: "Logan White Horse" $110-130.

Centre: "Watson's" $450-500.

Centre right: "White Horse" $60-70.

Bottom left: "White Horse" $150-175.

Bottom centre: "White Horse" $120-150.

Bottom right: "White Horse" $170-200.

Page 120

Top left: "Watson's" $650-750.

Centre left: "Watson's" $1000-1250.

Centre: "Watson's" $1200-1500.

Centre right: "Watson's" $800-1000.

Bottom left: "Watson's" (tray) $250-300.

Bottom centre: "Watson's" (matchholder) $300-350.

Bottom right: "Watson's" (jug) $750-1000.

Page 121

Top left: "Watson's" $1000-1250.

Top right: "Watson's" $1500-2000

Bottom left: "Watson's" (tray) $350-400.

Bottom right: "Watson's" (jug) $1200-1500.

Page 122

Bottom left: "Auchentoshan" $1000-1200.

Bottom centre: "Crawford's" $550-650.

Bottom right: "Glenfalloch" $400-450.

Page 123

Bottom right: "King George IV" $800-1000

Page 124

Bottom left: "King William IV" $325-375.

Bottom centre: "Lang's" $500-550.

Bottom right: "Daniel Crawford's" $220-250.

Page 125

Top left: "D.C.L." $1000-1200.

Top centre left: "Daniel Crawford" $1000-1200.

Top centre right: "Daniel Crawford" $900-1200.

Top right: "Robertson's" $800-1000.

Bottom left: "Robertson's" $1200-1500.

Bottom centre: "BOS" $1000-1200.

Bottom right: "Four Crown" $1200-1500.

Page 126

Top left: "Glencor" $50-60.

Top centre: "B.L." $1000-1200.

Top right: "Munro's" $200-225.

Second row, left: "Wallace's" $60-70.

Second row, centre: "Glencor" $60-70.

Second row, right: "Mackinlay's" $120-150.

Third row, left: "Corio" $45-55.

Third row, centre: "White Horse" $225-250.

Third row, right: "Bulloch Lade" $225-250.

Bottom left: "Corio" $20-25.

Bottom centre: "Bass" $300-350.

Bottom right: "Corio" $80-100.

Page 127

Top left: "Mackie's" $1200-1500.

Top centre: "Encore" $1000-1200.

Top right: "Mackie's" $1500-2000.

Bottom left: "Williams's" $600-700.

Bottom right: "Haig's" $4000-5000.

Page 128

Top left: "Bass & Co." $250-300.

Top centre: "Bass" $300-400.

Top right: "Bass & Co." $400-450.

Bottom left: "Bass & Co." $1500-2000.

Bottom centre: "Bass & Co." $1000-1200.

Bottom right: "Bass & Co." $1000-1250.

Page 129

Top left: "Flower's" $400-450.

Top centre: "Brakspear's" $400-450.

Top right: "Brakspear's" $90-120.

Centre left: "Dog's Head" $750-850.

Centre right: "Bull Dog Guinness" $2500-3000.

Bottom left: "Bull Dog" $900-1100.

Bottom centre: "Bull Dog" $1500-2000.

Bottom right: "Bull Dog" $800-1000.

Page 130

Top left: "Bentley's" $700-900.

Top right: "Powell's Ales" $2000-2500.

Bottom left: "Bailie Nicol Jarvie" $700-800.

Bottom right: "Double Diamond" $400-450.

Page 131

Top left: "Charrington's" $750-850.

Top centre: "Charrington's" $500-550.

Top right: "Charrington's" $450-500.

Centre left: "Rogers'" $300-350.

Centre: "Aston Ales" $400-450.

Centre right: "Cannon Imperial" $550-650.

Bottom left: "Courage's" $500-550.

Bottom centre: "Courage" $375-425.

Bottom right: "Courage's" $500-550.

Page 132

Top left: "Lincoln's" $600-700.

Centre left: "Tooheys'" $2500-3500.

Centre right: "Four X" $400-500.

Bottom left: "Perkins" $1200-1500.

Bottom centre: "Castlemaine" $800-1000.

Bottom right: "Perkins" $1200-1500.

Page 133

Top left: "Carbine Invalid Stout" $800-1000.

Top centre: "Queen Lager" $750-850.

Top right: "Perkins" $800-1000.

Centre: "Kalgoorlie Brewery" $750-850.

Centre right: "Kalgoorlie Brewery" $750-850.

Bottom left: "Tooheys Ale" $400-500.

Bottom right: "Tooheys Ales" $400-500.

Page 134

Top left: "Magee Marshall" $125-150.

Top centre: "Marston's" $800-1000.

Top right: "Mitchells & Butlers" $500-600.

Centre left: "Whitbread's" (matchholder) $500-600.

Centre: "Whitbread's" $450-550.

Centre right: "Whitbread's" (matchholder) $500-600.

Bottom left: "Whitbread's" $450-500.

Bottom centre: "Whitbread's" $450-500.

Bottom right: "Whitbread's" $550-650.

Page 135

Top left: "South African Brewery" $600-800.

Top centre: "Mansfield Ales" $500-600.

Top right: "Salt's Pale Ale" $500-600.

Centre left: "Worthington" $350-450.

Centre: "King George V Worthington" $450-500.

Centre right: "Worthington" $450-500.

Bottom left: "Foster's Bugle Brand" $800-1000.

Bottom centre: "M.B. Foster & Sons" $3000 plus.

Bottom right: "M.B. Foster & Sons" $450-550.

Page 136

Top left: "Friary Ale" $250-300.

Top centre: "Tusker Beer" $300-350.

Top right: "Worthington" $200-230.

Centre left (top): "Bass" $150-200.

Centre left (bottom): "Border - Prince of Ales" $65-75.

Centre: "Worthington E." $75-90.

Centre right (top): "Tavern Keg Bitter" $100-130.

Centre right (bottom): "Ind Coope's" $250-300.

Bottom left: "Ind Coope's" $350-400.

Bottom centre: "Greene King" $250-300.

Bottom right: "Truman's" $400-450.

Page 137

Top left: "Wm Younger" $250-300.

Top centre: "William Younger" $250-300.

Top right: "Wm Younger" $250-300.

Centre: "Young & Co.'s" $650-750.

Centre right: "Worthington's" $2500-3500.

Bottom left: "William Younger's" $250-300.

Bottom centre: "Wm Younger's" (figure) $450-500.

Bottom right: "William Younger's" $250-300.

Page 138

Top left: "Bombay Gin" $150-200.

Top centre: "Lamplighter Gin" $90-110.

Top right: "Beefeater Gin" $55-65.

Centre left: "Martel Brandy" $125-150.

Centre: "Bacardi" $60-70

Centre right: "Tanqueray Gin" $70-80.

Bottom left: "Beenleigh Rum" $400-450.

Bottom centre: "Beenleigh Rum" $700-800.

Bottom right: "Beenleigh Rum" $700-800.

Page 139

Top left: "Otard's" $500-600.

Top right: "Bisquit's Brandy" $900-1200.

Bottom left: "Milne's" $200-250.

Bottom centre: "Hamilton Ewell Wines" $1000-1200.

Bottom right: "Graham's" $350-400.

Page 140

Top left: "Historical Cellars" $20-25.

Top centre: "Broadways Shoe Store" $800-1000.

Top right: "Mildara" $25-35.

Centre left: "Sitmar Line" $70-80.

Centre: "T. Mewing" $400-450.

Centre right: "B.O.A.C." $75-85.

Bottom left: "John Player" $50-65.

Bottom centre: "Embassy" $40-50.

Bottom right: "Planters" $40-50.

Bibliography

Westcott, David: *"Australiana & Colletables"* auction catalogues, back issues from issue number ten, April, 1994 to issue number thirty, September, 1999.

Blakeman, Alan: *"BBR Auctions,"* various catalogues from February, 1993 to September, 1999.

Roberts, Warren and Thin, Laurie: *"Kiwi Auctions,"* various catalogues from 1997 to April, 1999.

Hill, Robin A.: *"A History of A.W. Buchan & Co. Ltd., Potters, Portobello,"* printed by Pandaprint, Dunfermline, 1997.

Westcott, David: *"Westcott Price Guide to Advertising Water Jugs,"* published by David Westcott in 1991.

Morrice, Phillip: *"Schweppes Guide to Scotch"* published by Alphabet & Image Ltd., Sherborne, Dorset, England in 1983.

Other books by David Westcott:

1986: "Australiana & Collectables Price Guide"

1995: "Carters Australiana & Collectables Price Guide"